THIS PLACE ON THIRD AVENUE

. . .

THIS PLACE ON

THIRD AVENUE

The New York Stories of

JOHN McNULTY

Memoir by Faith McNulty

Photographs by Morris Engel

COUNTERPOINT WASHINGTON, D.C.

The contents of this book were selected and edited
by Christopher Carduff of Counterpoint Press in
collaboration with Faith McNulty.

Library of Congress Cataloging-in-Publication Data
McNulty, John.
This place on Third Avenue : the New York stories of
John McNulty / John McNulty ; with a memoir by Faith
McNulty.
p. cm.
ISBN 1-58243-117-5 (alk. paper)
1. New York (N.Y.)—Social life and customs—Fiction.
I. McNulty, Faith. II. Title.
PS3525.A2847 A6 2001
813'.52—dc21 00-065863

FIRST EDITION

Book design by David Bullen Design

Printed in the United States of America on acid-free
paper that meets the American National Standards
Institute Z39-48 Standard

COUNTERPOINT
P. O. Box 65793
Washington, D.C. 20035-5793

Counterpoint is a member of the Perseus Books Group.

Contents

John as he was

     I met John McNulty on Valentine's Day 1941, in the City Room of the New York *Daily News*, where John was a rewrite man. It was the first day of my first job. John later told me that when he saw me he walked over to one of his friends and made a small joke. "That girl," he said, "will someday be known as McNulty's folly." Four years later we were married, and we were together until he died in 1956. After John died I didn't reread his work. I'd lived with the writing of it and knew it by heart. Now, after all these years and a whole other life, I have just read it again and once again and, as I did throughout the years we were married, find myself trying to find words to define this complicated, elusive, sometimes heartbreaking man.

I can still see the enormous City Room filled with desks, typewriters, telephones, and men in shirtsleeves. Next to the horseshoe-shaped City Desk were the desks of the rewrite men who turned raw facts, telephoned in by reporters working on the street, into stories that appeared in the paper. Rewrite men were the class act of the City Room, and John was one of the best. Taking a story, headphones clamped over his ears, he made a few notes, then wrote the story without any apparent pause for thought. Rewrite men have to get it right the first time—no fiddling with leads or leaving awkward sentences to be fixed later. As he finished a page he'd call "boy" and a copy boy, or girl, would hurry to take the page to the City Desk. I was a copy girl and found it thrilling to carry newly minted words from desk to desk.

One day, during a lull in my errands, John called me over and handed me something else, a proof of a story that had just been accepted by *The New Yorker*. It was a vignette, entitled "Atheist Hit by Truck," in which he captured a small event in big-city life. Although I didn't quite understand the story, which was in a form that was new to me, I was filled with awe at being so close to that illustrious magazine. I was also taken by surprise that he wanted me to read it. Looking back I can now see that this story was the beginning of a new phase in John's life. He had found his form and within a year was writing regularly for *The New Yorker*, joining the elite group of writers whose talent, skill, and grace made the magazine of the 1940's a thing of beauty and elegance from cover to closing period.

I would like to describe John as he was when I met him in the City Room of the *Daily News*, but he is hard to get on paper. What was most distinctive, almost startling about him was his eyes. They were of a blazing blue, with a wide-open, direct gaze. His hair was true black, his features rough and masculine with a nose that had taken a beating in barroom fights. He was not handsome in any conventional way, but he was magnetic. When he walked through a room, strangers noticed him. His voice was a beautiful, deep baritone with a lot of music in it.

The "place on Third Avenue" where McNulty found many of the stories in this collection was a saloon on the corner of Forty-fourth Street in New York presided over by Tim Costello and his brother Joe. It was an old-fashioned place even in 1942 when I first saw it: definitely a saloon, not a bar or restaurant, and with the standard saloon features— a long mahogany bar with mirrors on the wall behind it, shelves loaded with polished glasses, and tiles on the floor. The most visible evidence that it was different from other saloons was a mural—a series of large-scale cartoons of men, women, and dogs—with which James Thurber had decorated the long stretch of wall opposite the bar. Beneath the mural was a row of booths, maybe six or eight, for dining. John took me to Costello's for dinner the first time we met away from the City Room. A bit later on, Tim was the first of his friends that John introduced me to. It was early in the day, a quiet time, and Tim was sitting on a bar stool with a cup of tea and a newspaper. Without warning me, John pulled me over to Tim and said, "Look at her, Tim! I'm crazy in love with this girl!" Tim's eyes opened in surprise. He smiled and mumbled some sort of blessing. I realized later on that John would not have said something so intimate to anyone but Tim.

What made Costello's different from other Irish saloons stemmed from Tim himself, whose presence had somehow made the place into a salon as well as a saloon. He often worked behind the bar, with a white apron tied with strings about his middle. He was a big upright man from Ireland with shrewd blue eyes and a mouth that tended to be slightly pursed. It was the expression of a man who sees everything, but withholds comment. When he was amused his smile went wide, his eyes sparkled under bushy eyebrows, and he would polish the glass he was drying even more vigorously. He was a man of dignity and pride who disliked anything phony, especially phony Irishmen. John told me how Tim had disposed of one such St. Patrick's Day patriot who stood at the bar, flushed with drink and wearing kilts. Tim gave him a withering glance and said, "Pull up your socks, Hiawatha!"

A good saloon, John once wrote, should be a retreat from, and a miracle drug to alleviate, loneliness. "There is 'Parkinson's disease,' and 'Bright's disease,' and so on," he wrote, "but loneliness is 'Everybody's disease' . . . the simple, everyday loneliness, which makes it so nobody especially wants to have lunch alone."

Tim understood that, and his saloon was a place where a

man could always find someone to talk to without appointment, or could stand at the bar exchanging news and comments with Tim as he moved up and down it pouring drinks. Tim himself was not an easy-going man, but he believed that a saloon should be a low-key place, a neutral zone of relief from the pressures of the outside world. He succeeded in keeping Costello's that way until, ironically, John's writing about it, Thurber's murals, and the patronage of other *New Yorker* writers made the place famous. By the early 1950's Madison Avenue ad men were crowding in and changing the tone. John recorded the change in a line in a story: "Nobody goes there any more. It's too crowded."

I was twenty-three when I met John. He was forty-six. He had grown up in Lawrence, Massachusetts, in a neighborhood of Irish immigrants. His father was a bricklayer, born in County Clare, his mother a seamstress, from County Mayo; they met when she made him a suit. John was born in 1895, and his brother, William, two years later. Soon after, there was a sudden disaster. John's father fell from a factory chimney he was building and was killed. The widow's brothers came to her aid. They took up a collection and bought her a candy store. She and the boys lived in the back rooms, and the store's small proceeds supported them well enough.

John remembered the candy store lovingly—the liveliness of people coming and going, the greetings, bits of news and pleasantries, and never a moment of loneliness, at least in his recollection. All his life he was happiest with people around on just that level—not too long or too intimately.

It was John's mother who gave John the brilliant eyes and the talent. She was quick and witty, a wicked mimic who would "take off" the mannerisms of her customers after the door closed behind them. (John was an actor, too. He could charm a roomful of people by acting out stories and anecdotes.) Having grown up almost entirely among Irish people he had strong and conflicting feelings about them. He believed that they are separate and different from any other people. As he once wrote:

> The Irish are a dreadful race to be a member of
> When it's spring and your life you're in the
> > September of.

There was much in his Irish background that he wanted to escape and much he knew he never could. When we were setting off for a visit to Ireland, he was full of apprehension about how he, an Irish-American, would be received. He feared mockery. "They can be terrible," he said, meaning that there can be bitter wit hidden beneath Irish charm.

John got through school without giving it much thought, and began to work for the local paper, with a night job playing the piano in Boehm's Café. He took to the saloon—the fellowship, the merriment, the showing off at the piano. He tasted whiskey and loved that, too. He went on to college at Holy Cross, and then Colby, in Maine, but the excitement of war overcame him and he left to enlist in the Army. By May 1918 he was in France. His regiment, the Thirty-ninth Infantry, was in heavy fighting immediately. He was made a sergeant on the battlefield because, he said, all the real sergeants had been killed. He lived through Château-Thierry in July, but in August, at Vesle, he was badly shot up in the legs. Years later he wrote a story, "Two People He Never Saw," about the soldier who picked him up on the pitch-black battlefield and carried him to an aid station. John never saw his face and always wondered about the man who had saved his life. The other person in the story was a woman on the far side of the wall of John's dreary furnished room at a low point in his life. When *The New Yorker* published the story in 1944, the editor, Harold Ross, sent him one of his commending notes: "Your Christmas story was wonderful and as good a Christmas story as any magazine could possibly deserve."

Back in the States John spent a year in the hospital. There were deep scars on his legs that made him ashamed ever after to wear bathing trunks. He had a slight limp. Once, in the City Room, someone innocently referred to it and John flew into a rage. His vanity and pride of person were intense.

After discharge from the Army John went to New York,

where he studied journalism at Columbia but spent more of his time drinking with friends. He described it as a wild, wonderful, irresponsible time. Wounded soldiers could get away with a lot. He sold his Army-issue clothes for drinking money and went back to the Army store for more free clothes. He remembered fondly a rich old lady who bought these young heroes hot chocolate at Rumpelmayer's. He was young and strong enough to drink and do a day's work too. He found newspaper jobs easily and became known in the trade for speed and excellence, but there is little tolerance in city rooms (writers, like actors, have to perform on schedule) and he was repeatedly fired for drinking and bad behavior. Finally his friends decided it was time he left town. When he lost his job at yet another paper, somebody wired the editor of the *Ohio State Journal* in Columbus informing him that they were sending out a first-class rewrite man who should be met at the train station. They put John aboard with nothing in his pocket except a pack of Sweet Caporal cigarettes. He always remembered the misery of sobering up on the train and realizing his situation. He arrived humbled and ready to go to work.

In Columbus John was sufficiently sober and industrious to become a star, but he found the Middle West joyless and never lost his sense of exile from New York. To his good fortune and delight he found a comrade in James Thurber, who was a reporter on the rival paper, the *Dispatch*. They understood each other's jokes, which were often of a sort then unknown in Columbus. "Jimmy looked up to me," John told me, "because I was a writer from the big city of New York. He thought I must be worldly. He didn't stop to wonder why, if I was so sophisticated, I was there in Columbus, Ohio." Years later Thurber wrote about John: "He was not merely an amusing companion; he was one of the funniest of men. When he told a tale of people or places, it had a color and vitality that faded in the retelling by anyone else." John and Thurber saw each other almost every day. "He was invariably excited about something, the cabin lights of the *Shenandoah* [a dirigible], which he had seen twinkling in the sky the night before, a girl at the James Theater who sang 'Roses Are Shining in Picardy,' Donn Byrne's novel *The Changeling*, which he demanded that I begin reading right away, there on that crowded corner, or a song called 'Last Night on the Back Porch,' which he insisted on playing for me, then and almost there. Actually, he took me around the corner to a music store and began beating out the song on the first piano he came to."

Thurber also recalled that, when he and John had a falling out over some minor matter, John "was capable of a fine anger . . . sometimes as unreasonable as it was quick." They developed a manner of making up afterward, a running gag, during which the cause of the trouble was never mentioned. "Spotting him in a bar, I would present myself, politely, as a man just in from Columbus, Ohio, with a letter to him from Sully [a boxer they both admired]. 'Let me see the letter,' he would say, and there ensued a search through all my pockets, in which he helped. 'Let me have another go at your coat,' he would say grimly, but the letter was never there. 'Well, when you find it,' he would say, 'bring it around. If I'm not here, I'll probably be somewhere else. Meanwhile, let's have a drink to old Sully.'"

Thurber introduced John to a young woman named Donia Williamson and they were married in 1924. John moved from the *Journal* to the Columbus *Citizen*, where he was editor of the drama page and his name became well known. In those days whiskey was an integral part of newspaper life. The moment a day's work was done a newspaperman headed for the bar. For some of them, John included, this evolved into a drink in the morning to get going and a pint wrapped in brown paper in the desk drawer during the day. At last, John's drinking caught up with him and took over his life. There was one job disaster after another. He was forced into exile in Cleveland and finally in Pittsburgh, Pa., which is the newspaper equivalent of Siberia. Once when he was fired for drinking, he presented himself at the editor's desk the next day, sober, and with straight-faced formality said, "I understand there is a vacancy on the staff. I would like to apply for the position."

John was forgiven, but finally forgiveness ran out, even

from Donia, who divorced him. There was a period of living in furnished rooms. For the rest of his life furnished rooms epitomized for John the desolation and terror of true loneliness.

Meanwhile Thurber had gone to New York and was working for *The New Yorker,* a young magazine then, founded in 1925. He urged John to join him in the city and John did so, in 1935. It must have been then that he discovered Costello's and became friends with Tim. It was in Tim's that John made the decision to quit drinking forever. He told me about the moment when, standing at the bar, he saw himself in the mirror behind the rows of whiskey bottles and knew suddenly that if he didn't quit liquor he would become a drunk, a cadger, a permanent resident of furnished rooms. He raised his glass to his image and drank a last drink. After that, sobriety was his most precious possession. When we met he told me with pride that he had not had a drink in seven years.

Thurber introduced John to *The New Yorker,* and Ross hired him, but John's first stint there was brief. He wrote a few pieces, but the looseness of everything made him uneasy. He was used to newspaper discipline and the authoritative presence of an editor, someone to report to in the morning and to send him home when his work was done. At *The New Yorker* there were no hours, no requirements, no allotted tasks. Ross didn't give assignments; writers were pretty much on their own. St. Clair McKelway was managing editor. When John asked him what he should do next, McKelway would say, "Let's go and play a little pool while we think of something." John left *The New Yorker* for the security of the City Room at the *Daily Mirror.*

By this time Donia had returned and they had an apartment on Sutton Place. Sober, leading a structured life, his pride restored, John thrived. He had money in his pocket, and always kept a hundred-dollar bill tucked into his wallet for security. To fill the time that he used to spend drinking in saloons, he went to the racetrack and became a passionate two-dollar horseplayer. For John it was an innocent pastime that kept him out of trouble. As one of his characters explains, "It is one thing you can do by yourself and harms nobody." Horseplaying also provided stories. Betting on horses is for lonely men who run elevators and live in furnished rooms and eat in cafeterias with the *Racing Form* propped up. John understood them and at the track enjoyed their easy fellowship, which is part of the game. He loved the chance meetings and greetings, the talk that was warm but not protracted, and the stray remarks to be picked up. When a friend announced, "John, I'm having a wonderful day. I'm managing to lose very slowly!" John put the remark in his pocket, so to speak. I think of it now and then when something reminds me that I am getting older. I find it comforting.

At the time that John fell in love with me, he was living quietly with Donia. She had prudently decided not to have children; a dachshund named Tony filled the gap. Donia was a small, pretty woman, the same age as John. She was quiet and conventional, a true homemaker who kept everything tidy but shared little else of John's life. Neither John nor I had any intention of disturbing that arrangement, but, as time went on and we were still together, we became more and more deeply involved. Half-hearted attempts at separation didn't work. Then, in 1944, I was offered a job in wartime London and decided to go. John agreed. We parted with sadness and the intention of finality. The finality didn't last. John wrote wonderful letters and I answered them. Later I learned that on the day I left New York for London John had broken his vow and had a drink. He sobered up quickly, but the episode would prove a fatal breach in his resolve.

Meanwhile, John left the *Daily News* for a better-paid job at Time, Inc., and continued to publish stories in *The New Yorker.* His reputation rose quickly and he became one of the magazine's stars, along with such writers of that golden age as McKelway, Liebling, Mitchell, Hamburger, Perelman, Gibbs, Cheever, Thurber, and E. B. White, all of them friends of John and mutual admirers. His work attracted the attention of publishers and, inevitably, of Hollywood. In those days Hollywood snapped at any writer who appeared in *The New Yorker*. In 1945, while I was in London, John accepted an offer from Paramount Pictures to work as a screenwriter. Ross was chagrined. He didn't like having his magazine raided. "Goodbye and God bless you, McNulty, goddam it!" was his parting benediction.

John went to Hollywood, without Donia. He wrote me that he had told her he wanted to marry me and they had arranged to part. Since they were already divorced there were no formalities. I came back from London in September 1945, and we were married in Los Angeles at City Hall. Our married life got off to a rocky start. I think we were both somewhat shocked by what we had done and John suffered strong pangs of guilt over deserting Donia. Everything in our situation was disheartening. Postwar Hollywood was teeming with people looking for a place to live. I begged at real-estate offices, but the best I could do was two rooms in a truly seedy hotel. We hated the strange people, the endless driving, even the endless sunshine. Furthermore John's relations with the studio were going sour. "Paramount's lot is not a happy one," he wrote in a note to a friend. The studio had bought his stories about Costello's and wanted a screenplay based on them. The producers had apparently failed to notice that the stories' success depended almost entirely on language. They had no plot, no women, no sex, or much in the way of event. John had no experience in dramatic writing and had been set an impossible task. He was offended by suggestions that he depict his friend Tim as a comical Irishman. The tension and frustration became too much. John began to drink. The episodes were brief, as he fought the compulsion, but I lived in fear that he would disgrace himself at the studio. A very bad movie, whose name I forget, vaguely based on John's stories, was made somehow. John, having had a few drinks, insulted everyone concerned by walking out of the screening. Shortly after that, to my enormous relief, we were on the train to New York.

John was welcomed back with a contract at *The New Yorker* and also began to write a column on sports for the newspaper *PM*. His first book, a collection of stories called *Third Avenue, New York,* was published by Little, Brown in 1946 and got wonderful reviews. We lived in an apartment on East Seventy-second Street that I had rented before the war. John quickly made friends in the neighborhood—with Maxie at the newsstand, with Mrs. Robbins in the drugstore, with doormen up and down the street. His confidence restored, he established a routine and began to work.

It was a wonderful time to be writing for *The New Yorker*. With the encouragement of Ross, *New Yorker* writers were constantly inventing new forms of storytelling, new definitions of what is funny, and new ways of deflating the pompous and the phony. Each had his own style.

McNulty's was especially distinctive and hard to define. He could write a story so simply that it seemed as though he hadn't written it at all but merely transcribed what he had overheard. His language was not the language of literature but the casual talk of everyday people. He could snare spoken words like birds caught on the wing. His ear was perfect, his selections deft. He was considered a "humorist," but unlike his colleague Sid Perelman, for example, he was never cruel or sardonic. John's talent was in capturing brief, poignant, often ambiguous moments, and, in the words of one critic, "He did it kind of tenderly, without demeaning the people he wrote about." Unlike his contemporary Damon Runyan, who also found stories on the street, McNulty avoided sentimentality, or tried to. There was always an underlying note of feeling in his stories, something barely heard but as real as a heartbeat.

Though by the late 1940's Costello's was changing from an Irish saloon to a writer's saloon, John still found stories there about the nondescripts who floated in, and in Tim's always sage comments on them. Wherever he went John listened to the people he encountered—cabdrivers, bartenders, horseplayers, elevator men—all those who are usually ignored by people in a hurry. He could talk to strangers the way some people can charm children or animals, and he always seemed to have time for them. When he bought a newspaper on the corner he would have a word with Maxie, who crouched inside the kiosk, his pale, worn face half-hidden behind a pile of newspapers. John might ask if *Pravda* or *Izvestia* had come in yet. It was their running joke, and Maxie would light up with pleasure as he handed John the *Racing Form.*

John loved to collect bits of interesting language to weave into his stories. "He's Irish and he broods easy," a bartender said of one gloomy customer, and explained another by saying, "He is a cynic, and when he is drunk he don't believe in anything. You can't tell if he believes in anything when he is sober because then he don't say." John K. Hutchens, critic for the New York *Herald Tribune,* wrote that John possessed "an eye so sharp and an ear so keen, that they have few equals in American writing in our time."

I don't believe John talked to people primarily to gather stories but because there was something he truly needed in the touch of another human being. Usually what passed between them was no more than a small, rather innocent joke, but sometimes it was deeper than that. A cabdriver, telling John about his life now that his wife was dead, summed up his sadness with a quiet truth that John made the title of a story: "The Television Helps, But Not Very Much." Loneliness haunted John all his life and the small, brave strategies by which men strive to keep it at bay were often what his stories were about.

I've read somewhere that the French novelist Théophile

Gautier once said, "I throw my phrases into the air knowing that like cats they will land on their paws." John had little in common with French novelists, except that his words always landed just right. His singular, seemingly effortless way with words was admired by other writers. Joe Palmer, an erudite sportswriter on the *Herald Tribune,* wrote that "just as dogs will make up with some people and not with others, the English language will do things for Mr. McNulty which it will not do for the rest of us."

John did indeed love words. He read dictionaries, and he felt about the English language the way the French are said to feel about French—he hated to see it debased by sloppy thinking or careless writing. But he also admired the inventiveness of ordinary people, who told their stories in ways that might fail every grammatical test yet went to the heart of the matter at hand with a sudden astonishing phrase. A poem by Stanley Walker (at one time the City Editor of the *Herald Tribune*) that was published in *The New Yorker* attested to John's strong feeling for words. One verse read:

Don Skene and John McNulty, who are resting at
                                          my house,
spent most of the afternoon quarreling.
They do not like each other.
They almost fought when Skene advanced the idea

that "We can sleep all day tomorrow"
is the finest sentence in the English language.
McNulty held out for
"No date has been set for the wedding."

During the 1940's and '50's John wrote forty-odd stories and Reporter at Large pieces for *The New Yorker.* Other magazines wanted him too, and he did pieces for such magazines as *Vogue, Holiday,* and *Woman's Day.* A second collection of stories, called *A Man Gets Around,* was published in 1951, and again the reviews were admiring. John loved the praise and attention but success scared him. In a City Room, dealing impersonally with facts, he had been utterly sure of himself. Now, suddenly, he was pulling stories out of the air and was not quite sure how he did it. Each time the story seemed like an object found on the street, a piece of luck; having written it gave him no certainty he could ever do it again. He knew of course that his talent was himself. "I write the best goddam McNulty there is," he said, meaning that he had his own way of doing things and, for better or worse, this was what he must rely on. Publishers urged him to write a novel. John refused to try. He was careful to stay within what he felt were his limits. He never wanted to deal with strong emotions or troubling subjects. Orville Prescott, literary critic for the *New York Times,* wondered what a McNulty novel would have been like. "It might have been wonderful," he wrote, and noted with regret that John's "artistic modesty, his refusal to attempt a major work, meant that he will always be regarded as only a deft and delightful minor writer."

Life as a *New Yorker* writer was not easy for John. Without the routine of the newspaper he didn't seem to know what to do with all his energy and intensity. Writing a story at home, he would finish in half a day and wonder what to do next. I came to realize that John had been both blessed and cursed with more urgent emotions than most of us have to deal with. It was as though his feelings had less than normal insulation. He was sensitive to everything, sometimes on a level appropriate to a six-year-old child. When I picked up a nestling bird and was raising it, he was out of sorts. I asked him why. "That damn bird," he said. "You pay too much attention to that damn bird."

His pride was touchy beyond reason. A perceived insult was deadly and not easily forgiven. His likes and dislikes were quick and definitive. He disliked Rogers Whitaker because, on his first visit to John's apartment, Whitaker had laughed when Tony, the dachshund, became overexcited and wet the carpet. John was angry that his dear dog had been humiliated. In another instance, he never quite forgave Sid Perelman because, at a gathering of writers, Perelman directed his wit at one of John's simpler friends, who was defenseless in this fast company. John was never quite comfortable with people who were too witty, clever, and sophisticated. It wasn't his brand of humor. In some ways John was a romantic. There are no bad people in his stories. Bad people didn't interest him. In the City Room he disliked loudmouthed guys, the men who told unfunny dirty jokes that demeaned women. He was idealistic about women. He believed in the romance of Wallis Simpson and Edward VIII and was angry when a City Room cynic scoffed at it.

Though he didn't talk about it, I believe John was prey to anxieties and fears that he had to work hard to fend off. At the time of Pearl Harbor, he told me, he had been so overwhelmed by a flashback of fear that he thought he was losing his mind and went to see a doctor. The doctor told him to stay in bed for a couple of days and that fixed it. On the other hand, whatever he enjoyed he enjoyed immensely. His moments of delight were unalloyed; again, like those of a child. Getting dressed in new clothes, winning a bet, cashing the check for a story, finding a new friend, indulging an impulse to give our cleaning woman the money she needed for a set of false teeth—these things gave him unbounded pleasure. When he wrote about himself he always dwelt on the good times.

I suppose John's emotional intensity helped to entangle him with alcohol. He told me that his very first drink, when he was seventeen, was like falling in love. Years later, when he was determined to quit, he discovered on his own the principle on which Alcoholics Anonymous is based, that one drink unleashes an uncontrollable urge. He took great care to avoid the tiniest drop. During his life with me, John could go for long stretches without drinking, but sooner or later something in his chemistry would go awry. He'd become more and more tense and irritable, filled with anxieties and worries, and then, of course, he'd be unable to write. Finally, when the tension was unbearable, he would surrender. One dose of whiskey and his entire being relaxed, the color came back to his face and the sparkle to his eyes. Of course the good effects didn't last very long and the bad effects would take over his life. Dark, angry moods would surface, followed by guilt and despondency, which he tried to cure with more drinking. The cycle was hard to break. He would be helpless in its grip for days or even weeks. I came to see John as a man riding a headstrong horse. Sometimes he could control it, at others he lost the reins and couldn't stop it from bolting into the woods.

Writing for *The New Yorker* and *PM* John had no need to go to an office. He worked at home, sitting on the sofa with a portable typewriter on the coffee table and a cigarette burning in an ashtray. He made very few preliminary notes or tentative tries, but worked out the story in his head, then sat down and wrote at City Room speed, as though the devil were after him. At the finish he'd jump up, glowing with excitement. He wanted an instant reading. If I wasn't home he would call a friend and read it aloud over the telephone.

Before this John had always had a regular paycheck to depend on; it was part of what made life orderly for him. Now there was no certainty. *The New Yorker* was generous with a drawing account, but it was an advance against future earnings and had to be paid back. Money became a subject of great anxiety to him. I earned a salary and tried to convince him that we would always be able to pay the rent. It made no difference. John's feelings about money had very little to do with his actual bank account, which he couldn't keep track of in any case. His view of money was entirely emotional: money was praise in tangible form. Sometimes John borrowed money he didn't need from friends as reassurance of their love. At the same time he was unable to hang on to money. When he was feeling good he gave it away. When he was drunk he gambled it away. Financially there was no way to win.

Suddenly, in 1947, with no warning at all, John had a serious heart attack and wound up in a ward in Bellevue Hospital, New York City's famous charity hospital devoted to emergency ambulance cases and the indigent. I had been out of town. As I walked into this vast, and ancient, red brick fortress of misery, I was filled with dread, not only about his condition but also about the circumstances I would find him in. I entered a huge room, packed with beds. Ward B–1 was for male heart cases and whatever other victims of misfortune were picked up on the street. John was at the far end, near a high window that looked out on the East River, sitting up and joking with the man in the next bed. He assured me that he was getting the best of care. There were no frills in Ward B–1, no bells to summon anyone. What John found instead was a busyness and purpose, a casual friendliness, and a spirit of comradeship. Patients who were on their feet helped the attendants with chores, and the staff, though rushed, were kind and unstinting in their efforts. As days went by I realized that, strange as it might seem, John was quite happy in Bellevue. He was never in better form, charming everyone. When he got home he wrote a piece for *The New Yorker,* called "Bellevue Days," full of nostalgia for his alma mater.

Back at home John found it harder to adjust to his new vulnerability. He knew he shouldn't smoke, but he couldn't quit. He'd been told to be careful not to stress his heart by climbing stairs or carrying heavy objects. His response was to take wild chances such as carrying a typewriter up many flights to the press box at the top of Madison Square Garden, as if daring his heart to quit. When he was depressed he spoke of "the time bomb in my chest."

At the same time he was writing better than ever. He

wrote a long non-fiction piece called "The Jackpot," about a man who had won a radio quiz and the miseries that were visited upon him along with the prizes. Hollywood bought the story and we spent the money on a trip to Ireland. He wrote a story about the trip, called "Back Where I Had Never Been." Being in Ireland was an intense emotional experience for John. His feelings about Ireland were deep and strong. One day, on a street in Dublin, when I wasn't with him, his feelings became so overpowering that he had to tell someone then and there. He went up to a policeman and explained his need. The policeman understood.

A year after this trip, in 1950, came an event that changed both our lives—our son, Johnny, was born. John was thrilled with the baby, a man suddenly in love. A few months later I went back to work and a wonderful woman named Josephine Ellis became the baby's nurse and John's guardian angel. She was a large, handsome woman, dark-skinned, who radiated a kindness and competence that, like a soothing breeze, brought serenity to a room. The moment she arrived each morning the baby stopped crying, John became relaxed and cheerful, and I could leave for work knowing that both were happy in her care.

During the summer we often visited my mother in a quiet New England town, Wakefield, Rhode Island. After Johnny was born we bought a small farmhouse near her. John was at first highly suspicious of the country. He was a city man and professed to believe there might be a snake or a black widow spider lurking anywhere. After a while he found friends and his objections subsided. He hung out with the fellows at the news store and played pool with the town ne'er-do-wells at the local pub. He liked the beach club and enjoyed observing a type of person new to him— the New England rich and leisurely. "A Rhode Island picnic," he remarked to one host, "is where the butler wears sneakers." I have a letter from a friend, Ben Bagdikian, with an anecdote I like. Bagdikian, a newspaper man, wrote that he met John "at a clambake at the summer estate of some very aristocratic Rhode Island types. When it began to rain we had to retreat to a gazebo, where all the guests sat in a circle. One side was pretty much Junior League and Senior Junior League types, who stared in fear and wonder at the other half who were scraggly newspaper and writer types. In the awkward silence John said, 'When does the guy come in to read the will?'"

In Rhode Island, John kept in touch with friends by means of short notes. He wrote Thurber, "Dear Jimmy: I am on the porch of our farm house at 6 A.M. and there are some crows around. It comes to me what is the noise they make. That is, they sound as if they swallowed their chewing gum and are trying to get it up again. Yours, John." And again: "Dear Jimmy: My son Johnny, now 22 months old, ate his first clam one week ago Tuesday. Sincerely, John.

P.S. This is the only thing that has happened lately anywhere."

John had somehow picked up some rich-looking stationery from the Brook Club in New York and used it for a note to Red Smith. "Dear Red: I don't want you to think I am a member of this club, because I grew up in Lawrence, Mass., where my mother kept a candy store and we lived in the back of it and up to now no member of this club's mother ever kept a candy store where they lived in the back of it."

A card to E. B. White said: "Memo to E. B. White from Santy Claus: You have not been a good boy so I am giving your stuff to McNulty who is the ideal American boy. Santy C."

John began to write stories about Johnny that were too sentimental for *The New Yorker* but were published in *Woman's Day.* Some of them are love letters that are almost embarrassing to read, but are touching just the same. In one of them he wrote:

Dear Johnny:

I don't know exactly how to begin this and the way I figure it you don't know exactly how to begin living. That far, we're both in the same fix.

It's six o'clock in the morning and you are in your play pen . . . I'm having coffee and watching you, my first baby . . . There are many years between us, but they do not matter. You are my son, and I love you . . .

You are part Irish, Johnny. That is both a blessing and a burden. The bog and the wet wind and the poverty that are so far behind you have something to do with the kind of man you are going to be. You will probably be able to stand the wet wind and the coldness, but you will be hurt by sadness. I was. Not bad. But hurt.

You will be hurt by the sadness. The way people try to convey their liking, and try to belittle the hardships they have. If you give them half a chance, then it will come through, and the worst of all is the smiling sadness. Granted that I am not very clear at this point, Johnny, I hope it will get clear as we go on, as you get to be a little man I can take to the Yankee Stadium, as you get to be a little creature who will sit by me near the FM and hear music, a small lad who is my love and all, my little son Johnny. That's you.

A collection of these short pieces was published in 1955. I had mixed feelings about some of the stories, which seemed to me to cross the line, but Orville Prescott called the book "the truest and most appealing book about childhood you'll find this year . . . a description of the wonders of paternal love that is unique in its perceptiveness."

The little boy brought John tremendous pleasure. He spent hours with him every day, but Johnny also brought up troubling emotions. John had always been greatly bothered by the difference in our ages. Now he began to calculate how old he would be at each stage of his son's growing up. John was fifty-five when Johnny was born. When he was sixty-five Johnny would be just ten and want a father who could play baseball and do things like other, younger, fathers. John wrote a sad little story about how old he suddenly felt. As it turned out, John never got to see Johnny reach ten. He died just before his son's sixth birthday.

I don't know whether Johnny's birth had anything to do with it, or why it happened, but in those last five years John's control over drinking slipped more and more. Drinking made him sick, physically and in his mind, and it was a terrible thing to watch. I am sure that something in his chemistry was going more and more awry. There were many trips to sanitariums and places to dry out, after which he would be on his feet for a while, but John had an illness with no known remedy and he knew it. He never stopped trying to recover, but he was licked. In June 1956, his doctor told me, privately, that John's much-abused heart was failing rapidly and nothing could be done about it.

One warm summer morning I checked John out of a hospital for the last time in order to take him to our farmhouse in Rhode Island. Josephine and Johnny were already there. John was weak and subdued, grateful for being taken care of. In the cab on the way to the railroad station he said he would like to see Tim. We had time to spare, so we made the detour. It was noon and the place was quiet. Tim was alone at a table, having a cup of tea. He looked startled as he saw John, and then, as we sat down, I could see the shock and sorrow in Tim's face as he understood that this was the final farewell. We three sat together for a few minutes and talked about ordinary things. Then we said goodbye and went to the train.

At the farm, John tried to recuperate and to write. He started a story about eavesdropping on Johnny and Josephine. I found it later. He had stopped in the middle of a page with the word ABANDONED in capital letters and a note to me. "No, Faith, this doesn't have the right ring to it at all. Something's the matter with me, Faith, but I'll cure it. By God I'll cure it." A note he sent to Thurber was less sanguine: "Dear Jimmy: It seems that threescore years and ten is subject to change without notice."

Over the next fortnight, we talked about his getting better, but John became progressively weaker. He didn't fret or complain. His mood was one of quiet sadness. One morning he didn't get up from bed. He died later that day, the 29th of July 1956.

A collection of John's work, *The World of John McNulty*, was published in 1957. Thurber wrote a long and extraordinarily affectionate foreword. Stanley Walker wrote a review that began, "Many of the deceptively simple pieces in this collection are masterpieces," and ended, "He was a good reporter and one of the best and fastest rewrite men who ever lived. Even better, he was simply McNulty, which at its best was a fine and charming thing to be."

Faith McNulty
Wakefield, Rhode Island
January 2001

I.

This place on Third Avenue

This place is a saloon that grew up in the neighborhood, like one of the kids of the same Third Avenue block, between Forty-third and Forty-fourth streets. It is somewhat dim and dusty and it is run in a catch-as-catch-can style, with no efficiency at all. It isn't tough like some of the buckets-of-blood along the avenue, but practically everybody in here, customers and all, could take care of himself in a jam, each in his own way. This saloon has a good air to it, with no cheapness, although everything is plain and simple. The bar itself is plain, but solid. The wooden stools in front of it will hold you all right if you sit on them. The glasses are thick and large. These glasses, and the bottles, are about the only things in here that shine. The occasional sun is nicely screened through the benign dust on the windows, some of which look out on Forty-fourth Street and the others on Third Avenue. Occasionally the "L" rumbles by. There is an active serenity about this saloon, and somebody is always doing something, at least talking, all the time it is open.

Some nights when nothing happens are the best nights in this place

The boss of this saloon on Third Avenue often says he wishes there was such a thing as a speakeasy license because when all is said and done he'd rather have a speakeasy than an open saloon that everybody can come into the way they all are now. Not that he is exactly opposed to people coming in. They spend money, no denying that. But a speakeasy, you could control who comes in and it was more homelike and more often not crowded the way this saloon is now. Johnny, one of the hackmen outside, put the whole thing in a nutshell one night when they were talking about a certain hangout and Johnny said, "Nobody goes there any more. It's too crowded."

The point is that some nights when there's hardly anybody in a gin mill and nothing happens, why, those are the best nights in one way of thinking. They're more interesting and not such a hullabaloo of juke-box music and everybody talking at once and all of it not amounting to any interest for the boss or any of the regulars, unless you'd count a lot of money coming in.

Like the other morning about half past two it was more like a speakeasy, only a few there and odd ones coming in that the boss knew well and didn't mind any of them, each one different than the other.

Jack Yee come in first. The boss was having a cup of tea. He's a regular old woman about having a cup of hot tea down at the far end of the bar every now and then. Jack Yee is a favorite of the boss. Jack is a Chinaman that weighs practically nothing at all but he'll live to be a hundred easy. He starts out from Pell Street or Doyers every night around midnight and comes up Third Avenue on a regular route selling little wooden statues they send over by the millions from China. He sells them to drunks in saloons and about three, four o'clock winds up his route selling them in a couple night clubs.

The boss asked Jack to have a cup of tea, because he's always glad to see Jack. He can't understand how anybody could be as thin as this Chinaman and still keep going up and down the avenue night after night. Coldest night, Jack got no overcoat, just a skinny raincoat tied around him and always smoking a cigarette that's stuck on his lower lip and bouncing when he talks. So Jack put down his bag of statues and had a cup of tea with the boss, and first thing you know what are they talking about but how tough it is talking Chinese for a language.

You must know the boss come from Dublin and naturally has no hint of talking Chinese, but like everything else he has ideas about it just the same. It's no sense trying to tell how Jack talks but what he says to the boss is that there's the same word means two things in Chinese. Depends on how you say it, this word, high and squeaky or low and groaning.

Jack says *"loo"* if you say it down low it means "mouth." Then he tells the boss if you say *"loo"* up high it means "trolley car."

"Oh my God!" says the boss to Jack while they have their cup of tea opposite each other on the bar. "Oh my God, Jack, the same word mean 'trolley car' and 'mouth'?"

Jack says yes, and then he makes it worse by saying another instance, you might say. He tells the boss when a Chinaman says *"pee-lo,"* something like that, and says it low and moaning it means "a bird," and if he says the same thing high it means "come in!"

"Oh my God!" says the boss after another sip of tea. "The same word, Jack, mean 'come in' and 'bird'? And the same word mean 'mouth' and 'trolley car'? Then by God, Jack, if they're ever gonna make a start at getting anywhere they'll have to get that ironed out!"

With that, Jack is laughing because, like the boss says often, Chinamen are great people for laughing. They'd laugh if you shoot them. Fact is, he says that's what probably discourages the Japs, because the boss figures that Japs only grin but it has no meaning to it and Chinamen laugh from inside. They're great people, he says.

While the boss and Jack Yee were finishing their tea, they gave up the Chinese language as a bad job entirely, and at that minute who came in finally but the sour-beer artist to get his Christmas money and this the middle of February. The sour-beer artist is quite a guy in his own way. In this neighborhood they got a tradition that at the couple of weeks before Christmas there has to be written on the mirror back of the bar "Merry Christmas and a Happy New Year." The sour-beer artist goes around and puts that on the mirror. He does it with sour beer saved in the place for the purpose. You write with sour beer on the glass and it makes shiny crystals in the writing. Anybody could do it, of course, if he has sour beer, but this artist writes it with curlicues and that's the tradition that it has to be written that way. They give him two bucks and a half for it, but he's a fore-sighted guy and he can see ahead he'll be drunk and wandering by Christmas and likely in trouble, so he leaves the two bucks and a half unpaid some places to collect it after Christmas, when he's broke and hungry. That's why he just come in the other night, to get the two and a half, and of course he was welcome. Turned out he got a little stretch on the island for fighting around New Year's and here he was, sober and hungry. So the boss gave him the dough and threw in some soup and a roast-beef sandwich, and out went the sour-beer artist, saying to the boss, "Thanks, Tim. I'll see you around Christmas time." And it is true for him that's about when he'll show up, no questions asked, in time to write the curlicues on the mirror. In some ways the sour-beer artist is a little unusual, but that's the kind comes in on the quiet nights nothing happens.

Giving out the Christmas money to the sour-beer artist moved things back to Christmas for a few minutes in the place, and the boss got started into giving quite a speech on Christmas.

"I'm glad it's over, with office parties for Christmas starting unpleasantness," the boss says. "I mean I worry every Christmas about those office parties they have around here. Somebody always goes too far at them being chummy with the boss of their office, maybe one of the girls kissing him and then wondering for months afterward did she go too far. But Christmas is over and done with. The thing I remember about this one was something that I had a chance to sit back and have nothing to do with it. I was on a train going up to see a nephew of mine in a seminary a little ways up in the state and it was Christmas Eve. Well, first of all, it's the bane of my life around here that if a drunk gets to be a nuisance, by God it is always another drunk only not so far gone that thinks he can handle him.

"A thousand times in here I've seen a man beginning to drive out other customers by noisiness, or butting in, or something like that—well, I'd just have my mind made up I'd do something about him, even throw him out cautious if necessary. And that minute, without fail, up would come another less drunk drunk and say, 'Lemme handle him! I can handle this cluck!' That's the horror of 'em all, because then you got two drunks instead of one.

"On the train, in come this guy with bundles and his overcoat half on half off, and the minute he got on I shrunk back in my seat. I ran into them like that so many times, I was thanking God I was not in it at all and it was in a train and not here in my place. He begun singing 'Silent Night' and so forth and next nudging the guy in the seat with him to sing it, and then got sore because the man wouldn't sing 'Silent Night' with him.

"Then the drunk started changing seats like they change places at the bar here when they get like that. And he was by then opening up bundles and trying to show presents to a decent, quiet girl in the train. And hollering 'Silent Night' all the while. It was bad. And do you know anything about trains? The conductor won't throw you off if he can help it. They got rules the conductor has to get a railroad cop. That's because guys sues that get thrown off trains.

"Now up came the second drunk, the kind there always is. 'Lemme handle him,' says the second drunk to the conductor, exactly word for word what the second drunk always says in the place here. 'No,' says the conductor, but that wouldn't do. The second one grabs the first one, and by then we're pulling into 125th Street. And of course there's no cop on hand when they wanted him, the cop probably having a Christmas Eve for himself somewhere away from the station. Off goes the first drunk, the second drunk on top of him, the bundles half in the car, and the first one's overcoat left behind and the train pulls out. I gave thanks to God for once there was two drunks and me no part of it, because I've had it so often, even with the 'Silent Night' part thrown in for Christmas."

It was quite a speech about Christmas, nothing exciting but the boss was launched off on talking about it and it was one of those quiet nights nothing happens.

Still and all, Eddie Clancarty at the other end of the bar, drinking alone the way he mostly does, was trying to start an argument. He was hollering for a drink while the boss was talking about Christmas. People keep away from Eddie. He's quarrelsome. Came over here from the old country as a gossoon, and hardly made any friends because he'd take issue with everybody about everything. You can't say a word but what Eddie Clancarty would take you up on it.

"You bums, why don't you go into the Army?" Eddie hollered back at the other few in the place. "Why'n't you go into the Army?"

Without Clancarty hearing, one customer said to the

boss, "Why don't you throw him out, he's always starting a fight?"

"Oh, leave him alone," says the boss. "He's going into the Army tomorrow." He went up and served Eddie a drink, then got away from him quick.

Well, it got to be near four o'clock, time to put the chairs on top of the tables and close up.

"We'll go over to Bickford's and have some scrambled eggs when I get the joint closed," said the boss to a couple of the customers with him, saying it low so Clancarty couldn't hear. The boss likes to wind up the night in Bickford's having some eggs and some more tea before he goes home, and reading who's dead in the *Tribune* and having a look at the entries in the *Mirror*.

"What're you heels talking about?" said nosy Clancarty. But nobody answered.

"Drink up, Eddie, we're closing!" said the boss. Eddie hollered some more but drank his drink.

In a minute or two they all had gone out on the sidewalk, some waiting in a little bunch while the boss locked the door. Clancarty was cursing at nothing at all, just in general, and started away by himself.

"Let him go," said the boss, though there was no need of it, with nobody stopping such a quarrelsome guy from going. The boss and the others started for Bickford's, and

Clancarty was off the other way. The boss looked back at him going and said, "Now, isn't that a terrible thing? Sure I just bethought of it now! There he is, going into the Army tomorrow, and I can see plain as day what's the matter with him. The poor man has nobody at all to say goodbye to."

Two bums here would spend freely except for poverty

Nobody knows how the boss of this saloon on Third Avenue reaches such quick decisions about people who come in, but he does. Like in the case of the two bums who came in Sunday afternoon off the avenue.

It was that time on Sunday afternoon that the inhabitants of this place call the Angelus. That's about four o'clock when late hangovers from Saturday night come in one by one. They stay that way, too, one by one. Each man makes himself into an island, standing in front of the bar, and everyone keeps a space on each side of him the way water is on the sides of islands. These hangovers feel too terrible to talk to each other for a couple of hours yet, anyway. Each of them keeps staring into the mirror in back of the bar and saying to himself, "Look at you, you'll never amount to anything. You went to school and grew up and everything and now look at you, you'll never amount to anything." Old veteran Third Avenue bartenders call this fighting the mirror, and they all think it is very bad for a man. The place is sad and quiet when a batch of hangovers are doing this and so someone nicknamed this time of Sunday afternoon the Angelus.

The boss was tending bar himself. He was on the pledge again this Sunday afternoon, so he was standing behind the bar and not saying hardly anything. He is a sour man when not drinking, because he is a man who doesn't take very well to not drinking.

The two bums came in walking as if they had the bottoms of rocking chairs for feet. They had that heel-and-toe walk that punch-drunk fighters have that roll from heels to toes like a rocking chair rocks from back to front. They were never fighters, though, these two bums, too frail-built and no cauliflower ears on them.

They were scratch bums. In this neighborhood they call them scratch bums when they've got as far low as they could get, and don't even try any more to keep themselves without bugs on them. Therefore, scratch bums.

One bum had a version of a straw hat on him he rescued, most likely out of an ash can in a fashionable neighborhood. It had one time been one of those peanut straws they call them that look like a panama that's got sunburned, only cheaper price. The hat had a hell of a swaggering big brim on it, and looked funny over the scratch bum's crummy clothes. The other bum carried a closed cigar box under one arm, for God knows what and nobody ever did find out.

The two bums were arm in arm and they came in without making hardly a sound.

The boss took a drag on his cigarette and laid it down, the way he does when he's ready to tell bums to turn right around and get out of there, but the bums reached the bar before he did that. They come rolling up to the bar on the rocking-chair feet and one bum, the most sad-faced one, dredged up two nickels out of his pocket and slithered them onto the bar.

"How much is a glass of wine?" the bum asked, and even the hangovers heard him and looked surprised. Nobody ever asks for a glass of wine hardly in that neighborhood. Except maybe on Christmas Eve some nondrinker might unloosen himself up that much on account of Christmas. They keep wine only for show-off, so when the bum asked for wine a couple of the hangovers looked at him and so did the boss. He didn't seem to believe his ears, but he answered the bum. "Aw, wine is twenty-five cents," the boss said. He shoved back the puny pair of nickels at the bum.

"Oh!" the bum said. Just plain "Oh." He picked up his two nickels and him and his pal turned to go out. They took a couple steps toward the door when all of a sudden the boss yelled, "Hey, just a minute!" and wiggled a finger on one hand for them to come back to the bar.

Well, the two bums stood there, wondering what was

going to happen. The boss walked down to the other end of the bar and he reached back and got two of the best wine-glasses and wiped the dust off of them. He walked back with a hell of a flourish and set the glasses on the bar in front of the two bums. In this place they keep the imported stuff that's hard to get on account of there's a war in a little locker under the back end of the bar. The boss stalked back to this locker and out he hauls a bottle of imported Spanish sherry. Not the junk, a bottle of the McCoy, the real stuff, best in the house. He went to the bums and poured out two glasses full. Then he said, "Drink up, fellers, and welcome!"

You'd think the bums might be surprised, but they didn't look it. They seemed to take it in their stride like everything else. They lifted the glasses and drank the wine slow.

"Thank you, sir," the one with the big-brim hat said. "We won't be botherin' you any longer." And the two of them give their mouths a slow swipe with the backs of their hands and swiveled around from the bar and walked out. The bums looked dignified.

"Now, why in the hell did you do that?" one of the hang-overs asked the boss.

"Never mind why I done it," the boss said, grumpy. "Those fellers would spend thousands of dollars if it wasn't for they haven't got even a quarter. Only two nickels. Never mind why I done it."

The boss kept smoking his cigarette a while and paying

no attention to the hangover customers. After a couple minutes, damn if he didn't go down again to the far end of the bar and get his hat. He kept trying it on this way and that in front of the mirror.

"I wish to God," he said, "I could get my hat to set on my head the way that hat set on the bum. Now, didn't it have a hell of a jaunty look to it?"

Barkeep won't let anybody at all shove this handyman around

The boss of this saloon on Third Avenue was kicking out loud to himself one day about how things were going in the place and he said, "Nobody works for anybody around here." Well, they don't.

The help there aren't so many. There's Paddy Ferrarty the bartender, and Dinny the regular waiter, and Garabedian the chef, they call him Mike, and The Slugger. All of them seem to have hired themselves, and if there's firing to be done, they'll fire themselves when they get around to it and not before. The boss has nothing to do with it, practically. The gin mill gets along that way, after a fashion, and the boss hasn't got any feeling that he's authorized to give orders. He makes an occasional pass at giving orders but everybody goes on doing whatever they're doing in their own way, which generally is the opposite or at least a lot different to whatever way the boss told them.

The Slugger is the handyman. He tries hard enough, but the poor guy doesn't seem to be able to do one single thing exactly right, not one thing, although he tries hard enough,

God knows. So the way things work out, not being able to do one thing right makes him the handyman, entitled to take a whack at doing everything. Being a handyman lets him do all kinds of things, only all of them in a catch-as-catch-can style with nobody allowed to bawl him out much at any of the jobs because he's always only temporary at whatever the hell it is he's doing. He's a very temporary man.

Sometimes he's the waiter if Dinny don't show up. Now and then he's the chef for a few hours if Garabedian gets drunk and nobody can find him. When The Slugger is the waiter, he forgets to bring people butter. Then he mutters when they mention it. He gets mad because the butter didn't get there by itself and he feels that it is not his fault it didn't. When The Slugger is the chef, he does the best he can at it and he feels fine wearing the tall white hat that goes with the job. Only he is daffy on the subject of Lima beans and will serve Lima beans with everything you could mention, might even work them into the Jell-O if he could, regardless of what the customer ordered.

The Slugger weighs only about a hundred sixteen pounds, but they call him The Slugger because he talks very ferocious whilst drunk and he has big ideas about who he can lick then. He could lick hardly anybody at all. A customer one time said The Slugger looked like a guy that was maybe a small altar boy and fell into bad company for thirty-forty years. He is frail and got practically no health left from ramshackle living. Most of his teeth are gone and he must be nearly fifty years of age. Everybody likes this little guy, never mind his faults, they don't do any harm at all.

The Slugger believes everything he reads in the newspapers, especially about wrestling. Oftentimes, as a result of this, he stands in the middle of the saloon floor and tries to show single-handed, with no opponent at all, how Danno O'Mahoney worked the Irish whip. It's quite a strain on him. O'Mahoney was a big lummox of a wrestler and the Irish whip was a hold of his there was a lot of blather about in the papers a couple of years back.

Nobody pays any attention to The Slugger when he's talking big or showing wrestling holds, except Paddy Ferrarty, the bartender. Now it's a funny thing about a lot of Third Avenue bartenders like Paddy. They each got a kind of helpless little man to help them with odds and ends, and they treat him like a godson. With Paddy, The Slugger is such a little guy. He seems to Paddy Ferrarty to be like a fifty-year-old kid that has to be taken care of and people have to be blocked from picking on him or shoving him around.

Exavvy Mullane was saying the other day that this protecting The Slugger the way Paddy Ferrarty does can sometimes go too far, and sometimes it would surprise you.

Exavvy is a bartender that works in a bucket-of-blood up the avenue a ways and sometimes comes into this saloon to stand on the other side of the stick, that's what they call the bar around here. That's how Exavvy relaxes. Another thing that maybe better be explained about Mullane is his first name. His father was a rebellious, stubborn man, a thorn in everybody's side in the old country, and he noticed that hundreds of guys were named Francis Xavier this and Francis Xavier that. Mullane's father said the Xavier was the big punch in a name like that, so why not leave the Francis out of it entirely? There was quite a family fight about it, on account of some said it was sacrilegious toying around with a sacred name, but in the end Mullane got named Xavier Mullane, no Francis to it. So they call him Exavvy and sometimes just Zavvy Mullane.

Anyway, Exavvy was saying Paddy sometimes got the boss's hands tied in running the place with this watching out for The Slugger. "A couple of times I saw the boss tell The Slugger for God's sake wash the windows you could hardly see the 'L' through them," Exavvy said. "And The Slugger would walk toward the back of the place, his head hanging down, until he come to where Paddy was standing. 'What's the matter with you, did he say something to you?' Paddy asked The Slugger both these times. And The Slugger said, 'He told me to wash the windows again.' 'He did, did he?' said Paddy, sore as he could be, and marched up to where the boss was trying to look out through the front window to see if he could.

" 'Did you tell The Slugger to wash them windows again?' Paddy says to the boss as bold as hell. 'They're dirty,' the boss said. 'They're not too dirty at all,' said Paddy back to him. 'You're trying to kill that little guy, that's what you're doing. You know he's sickly and you'd be too. Sure the man has only et offhand for twenty years and the way he lives it's a wonder he's alive at all, and he can't sleep unless he'd be drunk in them cheap furnished-room beds, you got to put a lot of booze in you first or else the bumps in the bed would keep you awake all night. The Slugger's too tired and hard-worked to do the windows and for God's sake leave him alone.'

" 'Oh, all right, all right, let the windows go,' the boss says. 'Only don't be talking back to me like that.' Then Paddy says to him, 'I'm not talking back to you, it was me that began the talking.'

"Almost the same thing, word for word, happen twice, and of course it's all right with me, but you can see how it ties up the boss's hands. There's no sense in saying why don't the boss fire Paddy, because nobody gets fired here, and in the second place who knows the customers and their likes and dislikes like Paddy, how could you break in a fresh bartender to understand a place that's peculiar like this?

"Still and all," says Exavvy, "that was a great miracle, pradickly, that Paddy work out the time The Slugger collapse. It stands to reason he'd sooner or later collapse, with him so skinny anyway and no care taken of himself. It's come-day, go-day, God send Sunday with The Slugger. If he can chip in a half a buck with some other little guy and win a one-dollar bet on a horse, that's as happy as he can get. It's all the fun he has besides being cockeyed now and then, you might say. It's a hell of a life he leads, The Slugger.

"When he collapse that day it was a kind of parlay of a half a dozen things the matter with him that hit him all at once. The chef found him all slumped up in a booth one morning when he came in early. The poor Slugger's mind was a porridge of the war and submarines and racehorses. He was mumbling, with his eyes looking funny, and you could see he was sick from a dozen things at once. Some of the things the matter was not eating right all those years, and drinking, and bum sleeping, and God knows what. He kept saying it was five to one they'd torpedo Johannesburg, South Africa, which was the name of a town he picked up somewhere and the name sounded so fine to him he was always saying it. He was delirious, that's what he was. The chef took a look at him and called Joe, the cop that was out on the corner steering the kids across the street safe on their way to school through the trucks and the taxicabs.

"When Joe come in, The Slugger started swinging at him and muttering still about the torpedoes and something about it was six to one that Johannesburg would win the whole race. He was gone entirely, with the sickness hitting his mind. Joe the cop says he'll have to go to Bellevue. With cops, Bellevue is the answer to anything strange that happen, only of course in this instance he's right. The Slugger's delirious, no doubt about it. Off they took The Slugger to Bellevue.

"Paddy didn't come in to work till late that day and by the time he did, The Slugger was far gone at Bellevue. When Paddy heard what happened, he says, 'Oh my God, the poor little guy!' Well, they got hold of Father Carmichael somewhere and sent him to Bellevue to see The Slugger. In a couple of hours, Father Carmichael come back and he shook his head at Paddy. 'The Slugger's a dead pigeon,' says Father Carmichael. 'I don't mean he's dead yet, but there's no hope for him. It's no use going to see him at all, he can't recognize anybody, me or anybody else.'

"Paddy didn't do anything about The Slugger that day, and those who knew The Slugger or gave a damn kept waiting to hear was he dead yet. But it was the next day, with no word come, that Paddy went to the hospital. Before he went, Paddy says to me, 'I got an idea if I could get through to the little guy's brain or whatever the hell it is he uses for a brain, I might get him to pull out of it.' Well, I didn't say anything to that, and Dinny, not the waiter, the other Dinny, the cabman, took Paddy to Bellevue in the cab. He didn't throw the flag on the clock at all. Taking a personal friend to see a dying man, naturally he wouldn't.

"Dinny told me afterward about in the hospital. They had The Slugger tied down, but anyway he was so weak there wasn't any need of it. Paddy walk in, and even when he got up to the bed, The Slugger had no idea who Paddy was that took care of him for years, you might say.

"Then, the way Dinny told me, Paddy pull a chair up close to the bed and he lean right over The Slugger, who somehow kept still a minute or two anyway. 'Don't die, you little sonofabitch! Don't die, you little sonofabitch!' That's all Paddy say to him. Dinny say to me later he never hear anything like it in his life, how earnest Paddy said it, paying no attention at all to who else heard him, only making sure The Slugger could hear him.

"And with that, Paddy get up, shove the chair back, and says, 'Come on, Dinny, come on back to the place.' On the way back in the cab Paddy holler up to Dinny in the front, 'I think I got through to him.' That's all he say.

"Well, they come back and Paddy went to work, up and down behind the bar and saying nothing to anybody. Well, everybody knows The Slugger didn't die, because he's still around here. Fact the matter, five days after Dinny and Paddy was at the bed, in walks The Slugger into the saloon, teetering on his legs as if they were made out of ropes, but walking. Paddy grinned like an ape when The Slugger come in. He says to him, 'Hello, you wobbly little cluck,' and he told Garabedian, the chef, 'Hurry up get The Slugger something to eat.'"

They don't seem to be talking to Grogan

If the truth were known, and it is known to one or two of us, Grogan the Horseplayer has needed $300 for thirty-five or thirty-six years, possibly thirty-seven. He made another try at getting it last week, and this week he still needs $300.

Grogan, who is Malachy V. Grogan on his Social Security card, is as honest as the day is long but is also a horseplayer, as many bachelors who live in furnished rooms have a habit of being. He borrows quite often but never quite a lot. He borrows from the delicatessen man around the corner from his rooming house on East Thirty-ninth Street and he borrows even from the Greek flower-man up the street on Third, although how he struck up an acquaintance with the Greek flower-man is a mystery because the idea of Grogan buying a flower is preposterous. Grogan never bought a flower in his life; how could there be any occasion for him buying a flower? He only borrows from them when he is real stuck and then perhaps only two bucks to get through the night before pay day, or perhaps five bucks for some big affair like taking himself to the ice show in the Garden when it is there.

Grogan has peculiarities. If the Greek lends him a couple dollars or the delicatessen does it, Grogan is apt to tear the white margin off whatever paper is lying on the dresser of his furnished room and write down on it "Grk $2" or "Deli $2." He puts that notation in the watch pocket of his pants, and every time he changes from one pants to another, he never forgets to change the rumpled-up corner of newspaper with it, and one pay-day night or another, he takes them out of his watch pocket and walks up to the Greek's or the delicatessen and pays off. It stands to reason he must, mustn't he, else the Greek and the delicatessen wouldn't be going for it all these years.

But with the ups and downs of being a horseplayer, the scholarly-type horseplayer studying the *Morning Telegraph* through his thick glasses—Grogan is near fifty now, quiet, dressed almost sadly, his clothes are so dark and his ties so dignified and always a white shirt—with the natural percentage against him, Grogan always needs $300. He has a good steady job, pretty fair dough for a single man, even if it is no fortune of money, every week. Nevertheless, he has developed a faculty over these thirty-five or thirty-six years of being wrong a lot on who's going to win this race or that, so it all piles up to he could use $300 at all times. That figure always turns out to be what would have him sitting pretty, if he had it, whenever he has a studious night and sits down at the table in the furnished room and writes down so much for this, so much for that, and then adds it up, bearing in mind all the while that it'd be so much for this, so much for that only if he had what it adds up to—which, without fail, is $300.

What it is he writes down is things like "New Blue Suit $55" and "Send Present Godson $10" and "Go to Quebec Xmas $160" with a parenthesis behind it that says "(Don't Have to Do This)" and "Pay Doc for Tonsils $75" and the whole thing winds up $300. Grogan likes writing things down, and it's partly that which fascinates him about betting horses, in that he is writing down or making marks on the *Telegraph* half the night while he figures out the bets for tomorrow.

Over the years, where to get the $300 he needs has been quite a steady-going problem for Grogan. Of course, if things were different and the delicatessen or the Greek flower-man had that kind of money to lay out, why, they would let him have it, because they know very well he is honest as the day is long. But what's the use, they don't have that kind of money.

Who does have that kind of money is something that from time to time hits Grogan between the eyes, and no kidding about that. He has to go to work from Thirty-ninth on the subway or the bus, and there's hardly a subway car or bus that doesn't have this sign for Grogan to stare at while he rides to work or home from work. This sign is an ad. It says, "Do You Need $300?" It seems to be addressed right to Grogan for sure, even to the sum mentioned. The ad goes on to say that if a person needs $300, he should hurry up and come to the address given at the bottom and they will give him $300, which he can pay back at his leisure. The impression the ad gives is that the people who put the ad in the subway or the bus hate to see anybody going around without $300. They think it shameful to have anyone doing that while they are alive. Experience has not at even this late date shown Grogan that this is a wobbly impression the ad gives.

At the same time, the impression never seems to become wobbly with Grogan, so he made another try at it again last week and he told me about it while we sat around in Bickford's that night. Grogan said he saw the sign again that morning in the bus and again the same evening coming home and it gave the name of the nearest office where they give out the $300 and said they were open until 7 P.M.

"It's a funny thing but exactly three hundred dollars would fix me up nice," Grogan told me, as if he hadn't said the same thing years ago and often since. "So I went to my room and got washed up and put on my blue suit and a clean shirt to make an impression. That's one thing, too, came to me about the three hundred dollars, even while I was getting dressed to get it."

What came to him, he explained to me, was that he owed the Chinaman down the block $12.70 for laundry bills piled up over the last four or five weeks where he had a bad streak of luck with horses. The Chinaman, he said, is a good guy, a betting man himself that plays cards for chickens on Saturday nights with some friends of his someplace. He understands Grogan and trusts him and if he had $300 he might even lend it to him.

"It's twelve-seventy here and eight-ninety there and so on until I got it figured three hundred bucks would fix me up nice," Grogan said. "So I went to this office they said to go to, and I didn't have to wait a minute. The girl outside the door sent me right in and there was a very nice man waiting who took me over and said sit down. There were desks all over the place, nice and clean, and this man had my name from the girl because she asked what it was and so he said, the man said, 'Sit down, Mr. Grogan,' and I sat across from him. I been through it before, but this time it felt more successful.

"He asked me how much I wanted to borrow and I blurted out three hundred dollars. He didn't blink an eye. He asked what I wished to do with the money. That's what he said: 'What do you wish to do with the money, Mr. Grogan?' I said I wanted to clean up some bills I owed. 'Very wise, Mr. Grogan,' he said. 'Why be worried over trifling bills spread all out when we stand ready to help you clean them up at once.' That's what he said and things looked good. Then he said, 'Do you have a Social Security card, Mr. Grogan?'

"I took out my wallet and started fishing for it but I had to stand up to get it out of my pocket and when I fished into all the junk I carry in my wallet a lot of stuff fell out. This was a very polite man, I liked him, and he reached over to the floor to help me pick it up. What does he find but three small mutuel tickets I'd stuck in there last Saturday when I went out to Jamaica and I forgot about them because they were losers. He picked up the mutuel tickets and looked at them and he froze up and said, 'All right, Mr. Grogan, we'll call you.' I never see a guy change so fast. I was outside in a minute. When they say 'We'll call you' it's all over. The sign says 'Do You Need $300?' but they don't seem to be talking to me."

A man like Grady, you got to know him first

Some of the people that inhabits this saloon on Third Avenue requires explanation. Grady the Cabman is one of them, and the other night, for want of anything better to do, Paddy Ferrarty was trying to explain him the best he could and make talk anyway for a while while there was hardly anybody in the place.

"A man like Grady, you got to know him first," Paddy said. "Else you won't make any headway at all understanding a man like that. Grady befuggles even me sometimes, and I know him since they said then he was only about seventy. Some around here says he's around a hundred, putting it on a little perhaps, but he's anyway old. Maybe he's sixty-eight, but God knows. And God'll tell you sooner than Grady.

"The thing about Grady is he seems to be always doing two things that works opposite each other and spending all his time doing it. Like he takes a cab out of the garage every night and then he spends half the night trying to keep people from getting into it and making him take them someplace. If he don't want to have people in the cab, and God knows he don't most of the time unless he can pick out who gets in his cab, well then why does he take out the cab in the first place? That's the part about Grady, you got to know him first. And even then it ain't any too clear what Grady's all about. Maybe it ain't important.

"He only wears a wig when he goes to court, or did you know he's as bald as a banana? Well he is, but how hardly anybody knows that is he wears that cabby cap night and day, wouldn't take it off for anybody. You'd get him raving mad if you yanked it off his head. Never takes the cap off even if he goes into somebody's house—I mean into a friend of his's that's drunk and got to be carried in and help the wife get him into bed and his collar unbuttoned and his shoes off so he won't choke and can sleep easy.

"One day Grady come in here in the middle of the afternoon, which was surprising to see Grady in daylight ever. I happened to be here on account a cousin of mine was with me at a funeral and I had to get up in the daytime, and after the funeral I brought my cousin in here to show him where I work because he belongs in Brooklyn and don't get around much. Anyway, there was Grady wearing the wig and his cap off sitting at the end of the bar. He claim he found the wig one time in the back of the cab off a customer and it fit him, but so help me God I think he bought the thing. He explained why he had it on after he had to admit it was a wig, couldn't fool anybody any more than a wax apple. He got into some kind of traffic trouble, which don't happen often, I'll say that for him, and he had to go into court. He knew there's no getting away with keeping your hat on in court. Grady or no Grady, lifelong custom or no lifelong custom, take off your hat and no goddam arguments. So he wore the wig. The wig's unimportant anyway, but it's one of the things you got to understand about Grady and I'm only starting with the wig. It's hardly anything at all.

"The funny part is Grady got his own way making about three bucks a night with the cab. Even if he don't, he don't worry. You take the start of a nice summer night for instance here around Third Avenue, say take six blocks up from here and say five blocks down from here. Well, that makes eleven blocks in all and in eleven Third Avenue blocks it stands to reason they got a slather of saloons.

"Well, we'll say it's the start of a fine summer night around here. Maybe seven o'clock and the 'L' is roaring down from time to time and some kids standing in a bunch on a stoop on the side street and singing 'Don't Sit Under the Apple Tree with Anybody Else But Me Till I Come Marching Home,' and the little guy, they call him Shorty, smoking a cigar on the corner, God knows where he gets all the cigars, and everything like normal for the start of a fine summer night and along comes Grady.

"He starts sizing up the terrain as they say. He puts the cab at the corner, facing the wrong way chances are, and he walks a ways smoking that dudeen of his.

"Calm enough, he goes into this saloon and he goes into that saloon along the line. Maybe he'll see Junior Connors lined up at the bar in the first saloon. He's a big fat guy with a fine rum blossom for a nose and looks nothing at all like a junior so they call him that. He's a regular customer or ward, or whatever it is, of Grady's. Wards is better. They're more like wards than customers. Grady chooses them, they don't have hardly any hand in picking Grady for a cabman, he takes care of them year after year. Anyway, Junior is like most of the guys Grady'll allow in the cab, you might say. They're nearly all fellahs that have good enough jobs to keep them in liquor money, works regular but mostly devotes themselves to drinking and singing and arguing. Not rum-dumbs but warmin' up to be rum-dumbs.

"Anyway, to get back to Junior, Grady takes a look at him beginning to drape over the bar. Grady got little squint eyes and some says he doesn't see good, but I think he can. He can spot Junior and the rest of them. A man that claims Grady can't see good any more claimed to me one time Grady drives up and down Third Avenue by memory and don't see much ahead of him. This man claim that's why Grady don't like to drive on the West Side, because he can't remember it and don't see it, and the same guy claim it's a terrible thing for Grady they're tearing down the Elevateds because the way Grady drives he counts on the 'L' being there and it'll ball up his driving if the 'L' ain't. I think the man was exaggerating about Grady. He sees well enough I believe.

"When Grady takes a look at Junior, Grady says nothing, don't even say hello, but in his own mind Grady says to himself, 'Connors'll be ready by ten o'clock.' In other words he kind of make a mental note of Connors and the shape he's in figuring like an estimate the shape he'll be in by ten o'clock probably ready to be taken home. Then Grady leaves that saloon for the next saloon that's only no distance at all.

"In the next saloon we'll say Grady spots another regular of his, maybe Shauno Haggerty that already, and it's only ha-past seven, is standing there reciting 'Dawn on the Coast of Ireland'—I'm so goddam sick of hearing about dawn on the coast of Ireland from Shauno. 'Oh-oh,' says Grady to himself, making a mental note of Shauno, 'he'll be the first, he's almost ready already. I'll get him home first, soon as I take a look around the other places.' Out goes Grady and to the next adjoining gin mill.

"That's the way Grady does. In a half hour after he gets the cab parked on the corner, and a trip made into the saloons, he's kind of got himself booked for the night. You know how I mean—he's got to take Shauno at eight o'clock and steer him into the cab and home, then Junior at ten o'clock, and some other guy he's spotted will be drunk and ready at one o'clock, and so on.

"When these times come it sometimes gives me the shudders to see Grady circlin' around the guy he got picked to take home soon. He looks like a buzzard closing in on the guy sagging over the bar, but when all is said and done it's a good thing. Somebody got to take them home or God knows where they'd wind up and Grady takes care of them like a mother you might say. But a pretty tough mother it'd be running up nickels on a taxi clock taking care of her son, now wouldn't it?

"You can see in the meantime between these guys to be taken home at certain times Grady got fixed in his mind why he don't want a lot of strangers climbing in the cab. Grady gets into the euchre game, and the hack out at the curb bold as you please. I seen guys, strangers, push the horn and push the horn, trying to find the driver, and finely come in and say, 'Where's the guy drives this cab out here?', and all the while Grady'll be whispering loud out of the corner of the mouth, 'For God's sake don't tell him. Don't tell him for God's sake.' That's what he'd be saying to me, in deadly fear he'd be cornered into carrying a stranger around in the cab. You got to know Grady first to understand a man'd act like that.

"It ain't that he's surly, I seen him kindhearted often.

One time I had to climb in the hack, run an errand around Fifty-ninth. It was about seven P.M. and when I got into the cab what was in the seat but a scooter, two dolls, and three tops. 'What the hell is this?' I says to Grady. 'Oh, never mind them,' he says, 'the McNally kids were playing house in the cab, leave the kids' things alone.' Grady wouldn't stop kids playing house in the cab. He's kindhearted.

"But Grady's even worse than I told you about regarding the cab as a private affair of his own and not something for every Tom, Dick, and Harry to get into that's got a couple bucks and wants to be taken someplace. I've seen guys get into the cab while Grady was sitting in it, dopey, and not seeing them get in, and you ought to see Grady then. He steps on the starter without turning on the switch and it make a discouraging noise, whirrrrrrr, and of course the engine don't start. Grady looks around his shoulder at the stranger while he does this a few times and the stranger finely gets out and looks for another cab. Grady's tickled to death and turns back to reading the Intelligence Test in the *News*. The Intelligence Test is a favorite of his, especially if it's got geography in it.

"Grady claim he been everywhere but you can't tell where lies start in and the truth leaves off but you can be sure it's early in what Grady is saying because he's an awful liar. He claim he worked in shipyards everywhere. Whenever there's a war comes up, Grady's bragging about how he makes ships in the old days. Nobody knows, but this I do know. He disappeared one time four years. Four solid years. The way it happened Grady thinks nothing of it, but some would think it was mystifying. He sometimes takes little rides for himself to look at things, the way an old gentleman might take a ride for a whim to look at something. This day, it was years and years ago, Grady druv himself down to the Battery, he wanted to look at some ships going by, he thought at the moment he needed to see some ships for a change.

"Well, he went down there and four years later he came into the house up in the Bronx where he lives, and his wife and his kids were still there. One of the kids had growed up, you might say, in the meanwhile because this kid was fourteen when Grady took the ride to the Battery and he was naturally eighteen when Grady come back. That's the growing-up time, between fourteen and eighteen.

"Grady's wife seem a little surprise to see him, he told me later on, but no great fuss made. She must be quite a woman, or at least she know Grady. He said it was just dinnertime and one more for dinner in a house like that makes no difference so he pull up a chair. He told her he was working those four years in a shipyard in Clyde that's in Scotland, and that's all there was to it, those whole four years.

"I remember asking him what the hell he thought the

wife and kids would do when he just plain left the cab at the Battery, abandoned it, and saunters over, maneuvers himself onto a ship and to the Clyde. 'Aw,' says Grady, 'the wife have a rich aunt. They was nothing to worry about with the rich aunt sure to take care of them all soon as it dawn on them I'm gone for a while.' A guy like that Grady, how you going to understand him without knowing him first?"

Man here keeps getting arrested all the time

Grogan got arrested again Thursday. Talking in this place on Third Avenue Friday night, he said he was getting sick and tired of it. That's about the ninth time he got arrested lately. He seems to be having a streak.

Grogan is a nice, quiet little man. He bets on racehorses and thinks about them night and day. Mostly he gets arrested in raids on puny horse rooms around Third, Second Avenue, occasionally Lexington Avenue.

Grogan's a solemn, small, scientific-minded little man, with no laughs at all written on his dead pan. He comes by being scientific-minded honestly, because in Ireland his old man was a Latin scholar just for fun. That's how Grogan got his middle name, which is Vercingetorix. His whole name is Malachy Vercingetorix Grogan, but they call him Grogan the Horseplayer. It sounds like a trade, like bricklaying.

Getting arrested doesn't bother Grogan in his pride or leave any marks on his character. He manages to remain altogether aloof from the cops that arrest him. But what gets him sore is he says you miss your dinner when you get arrested in these raids. They almost always happen half past four in the afternoon and no Night Court to stick you in front of until about ten o'clock that night.

"I don't know do they folly me around or what, those plainclothes policemen," Grogan said. "But it seems lately no sooner am I settled down nice and busy in one of these horse rooms than along about the fifth race at Aqueduct in come the policemen again.

"They're decent enough when they come in on a raid, unless once in a while somebody in the crowd of horse-players shows signs getting tough. They have to paste them a couple then—not too hard—so everybody else will get the idea what's done is done and make the best of it and they'll know it's a raid. These couple of pastes in the jaw for somebody is what they might call in a show establishing a mood. The policemen establishes a mood that way."

This last arrest, Grogan said, just about broke the back on his camel. He got to brooding about it. Paddy Ferrarty, the night bartender, often says about Grogan, "He's Irish and he broods easy."

"It's heartbreaking the way I got to do now," Grogan went on. "They got me half scared of the little horse rooms, and I don't ketch holt of enough money for decent pool-rooms. I usually got seven dollars, only, to start with. Consequence is I'm playing with guys makes book in an auto on a corner. They sit in the auto and won't let me or the other horseplayers sit in it, naturally—ain't room enough.

"No, we got to stand in the rain or doorways to look at the *Racing Form,* and walk over to the auto and make bets, or get the results that comes in over the radio. You seen that kind of bookmaking. You can tell this auto, on a different corner around here nearly every day, because it has a sign on the front, 'Remember Pearl Harbor.'

"This last raid—I don't know, it got tiresome. I make out better than the other guys arrested. I'm used to it. Like when they're going to lead you out to the patrol wagon at the curb, nobody wants to be first outside the door and pass through the crowd. A crowd always stands around as close as they can to a patrol wagon, and the cops make a space between 'em, like an aisle outside a church for a wedding. But I got over all that bashfulness about going out first and let them gape at you. The hell with them in the crowd. You're not criminals anyway, only horseplayers meaning no harm, only want to win a couple dollars. And what the hell, the cops themselves ain't even mad at you; they got to make a couple raids every week to put in the records.

"And what I found out is you get across the sidewalk first and into the wagon and you get a seat. Why, the last time they had twenty-seven guys jammed in there, standing up, sitting on each other, piled up every which way, miserable. So I'm first across the sidewalk—let them gape—and I got a seat.

"First they took us in this last raid down to the police station on East Thirty-fifth Street. The whole twenty-seven in a big room and certainly a mixed-up bunch. They had guys like me, and wops, and some Longchamps waiters with red braids on their coats would probably get fired because it was five o'clock by then and they ought to be back to work. Three or four horseplayers had helmets on. Steel helmets. These helmet guys work in the slaughterhouse on First Avenyuh. They got to wear helmets because the big sides of beefs run along a conveyor on hooks and without the beefs the bare hooks sometimes hits the guys in the head. Therefore helmets.

"The way you mill around in that police station is an awful waste of time. Just mope there, but a guy sells coffee if you want it. That helps and he makes a handy dollar with all the prisoners dumped in there all the time.

"It's about six o'clock before they took us up to East Sixty-seventh Street, what they call Division Headquarters. They count you before they put you in the wagon and they count you up at East Sixty-seventh Street and they count you before they take you out of there. My God, you get sick of being counted! I hate cops counting me, but they have a slip says twenty-seven guys arrested and they deliver them around from station to station like merchandise. Another thing that's not becomin' at all is that in East Sixty-seventh they put you in cells. No matter who you are, getting put in a cell can make you sad, even if only for horseplaying.

There's something about seeing a man walk loose by the door and you can't walk loose but got to look through bars that sinks your heart out if you let it. Only I don't let it. The thing that bothers me is why do they go through all this at all, to say nothing of making you miss your dinner? Why do they keep bothering poor, simple, ordinary horse-players and turn them loose anyway in the finish, which they always do?

"It seems useless to me. I always thought now for years I love to study horses and bet them when I can because it is one thing you can do by yourself and harms nobody at all. I can be busy with horses, the *Racing Form* or maybe the *Morning Telegraph,* all winter nights and summer nights in Bickford's or in my room and never harm anybody, but they got to keep on arresting us. Getting married causes trouble, drinking causes trouble, working wears a man out, and I see guys all around me dying making successes out of themselves. Why can't they let me harm nobody just studying horses and playing 'em when I can?

"I almost forgot to say just before the raid I bet a horse at Suffolk, two dollars win, with Louie the bookie. But then the raid come, and of course they stopped the radio, gathered up all the *Form*s and all, and with all the moving from station to station I couldn't find out how the Suffolk race come out. None of the cops were watching me especially in the raid, and I snuck an Arlington Park part of the *Form* into my sock, folded up, and I had that at East Sixty-seventh Street. I could study that in the cell, and they run late out there at Arlington because it's in Chicago. Well, damn if I didn't find a horse in the last race out there I'd been watching for weeks. He could win easy, and luck would have it Louie walk by the cell and stopped there. He must have slipped a cop something and they broke him out of a cell and let him walk in the corridor back and forth—more comforting than in a cell. I asked Louie if he would let me bet the last at Arlington, although by that time the race was over. I didn't have money, but if the Suffolk horse had win, well, I could 'if' some money off him. That means if the first horse wins, you can bet some of the win on another one. It's like a contingency basis in the legal world, only it's 'iffing' in horse rooms. 'Honest to God, don't you know how the race come out at Arlington?' Louie asked me. 'Nobody told you, did they, in jail here?' I told him honest to God I didn't know. 'O.K.' he says. 'You're an honest guy, Grogan. You can have four win on the Arlington horse.' Then he walked away from the cell. They both win, it later turn out, and so I beat Louie for sixteen-seventy.

"I was glad I went out first to the wagon when they moved us to Night Court over on West Fifty-fourth Street. I tell you why.

"It was dark when they moved us, and of course the wagon was jammed up again. The seat I got was up front, and there's a round hole in the partition that divides the driver off from us. Well, as we drove along I could look through that round hole and see all the corners I knew. It was very interesting, just looking through that hole and seeing a particular building and figuring out 'This is Lexington and Sixty-fourth' or else 'This is Lex and Fifty-ninth.' The electric signs are blacked out, but I could read some anyway and they looked pretty through that hole and made me forget how rotten it is packed in a patrol wagon getting arrested all the time for doing no harm.

"Of course, they counted us again at the Night Court, where you stand around in a detention pen. I felt like saying, 'Stop counting me. I'm still one guy, the same as I been all my life.' But what's the use? The less said in a detention pen the better.

"The bailiff got me a little mad. They haul you up in a bunch before the magistrate, and when it came our turn, the bunch from our particular raid, what do you suppose the bailiff shouted to the magistrate? Well, he hollered, 'Malachy V. Grogan and twenty-six others!' I asked him, 'What's the idea singlin' me out?' 'Aw, you're here all the time,' he says. I let it go at that.

"They dismissed us, the magistrate did, the way he always does. We get charged with dis. con., they call it, means disorderly conduct, and there's a couple minutes' blather and they turn us loose, ten o'clock or so and no din-

ner yet. They hold Louie. They got him charged with main.
nuis., which is maintaining a nuisance, probably meaning
Malachy V. Grogan and twenty-six others. It all seems useless, and I don't know why they got to keep arresting us all,
not doing anybody a bit of harm but finding an interesting
way to put in all the days and nights.

"Louie give me the sixteen-seventy after we got out. He
got bailed in no time. I knew he would because Louie's the
kind nobody pens him up very long and so I was waiting in
Fifty-fourth when he come out. He bought a *Telegraph* at
the stand there at Fiftieth and Broadway and we found out
how the races we missed in jail come out."

The Slugger comes into his own

The Slugger had the good fortune to break his right leg one winter day. This started a chain of circumstances that made The Slugger a man among men. Not that he wasn't before that, because he was.

The Slugger is physically a small man. He is spiritually a large man. He is imaginatively a prodigious man, because he imagines himself, at times, to be able to conquer the most rugged wrestlers, to knock cold the most hardened prizefighters, and to cow the boldest employers.

The Slugger is a handyman, casually working first for this one and then for that one along Third Avenue between Forty-second and Fifty-ninth Streets. He works casually because that is his nature and because the kind of work he does is casual anyway. He might wait on table a little, he might cook a little, he might sweep up a little, he might do anything that does not require too constant application.

This winter night, The Slugger was making his way from McCarthy's, at Forty-fifth and Second (a block to the east off his beat), over to the home region of Third Avenue. Without assistance from himself, he stumbled and fell over a grating that was jutting up on the proper sidewalk. That was the beginning of his luck. When Joe, the policeman on the beat, picked up The Slugger a few minutes later, his right leg was all out of shape. Joe told him to sit there in a doorway while Joe called the ambulance from Bellevue. When they got him there, they found The Slugger's right leg was broken.

The Slugger took great joy in it. His friends heard he was in Bellevue and, learning upon further inquiry that he was not in there with the creeps but with a broken leg, they became very solicitous about him. They came to visit him one after the other. One brought a pint and stuffed it under the pillow, one left him two dollars in cash, another made it a point to bring him the *Daily Mirror* every day. The Slugger was a moderately big man right away.

When The Slugger got out of Bellevue, he was limping very picturesquely and walking with a cane. He had an expression of fortitude on his face when he got back to the old neighborhood, and everybody asked him how he was making out and told him they were sorry about his misfortune.

"Oh, it's all in the game," he would say, "it's all in the game. But, God, it hurts terrible in the damp weather."

It was getting on spring and April then, so there was lots of wet weather and The Slugger had opportunity enough to look up at the sky when he said how the damp weather made the pain worse.

One day, a lawyer came looking for him, not long after he got out of Bellevue. The lawyer went into Tim's saloon, which The Slugger had given as an address when "admitted," as the saying goes, into Bellevue. "Admitted" is a fine word for such a place; the way it sounds, a person would think it was an exclusive club. Anyway, the lawyer got the address of Tim's and came in there asking for Carroll M. Holligan, which was The Slugger's right name, although hardly anybody knew it but the Social Security people and the place in Ireland where he was born, baptized, and confirmed. That town was Ballyhaunis, in the County Mayo.

"I don't know where he is this minute," Tim told the lawyer, "but if you tell me what it's about, I might be able to find him in the next day or two."

"That was pure negligence, the occasion on which Mr. Holligan suffered a fracture of the right leg," the lawyer said.

"The Slug—I mean Mr. Holligan wasn't the least bit negligent," Tim said. "He was going along minding his own business and it was slippery and that grating stuck up unbeknownst to him."

"I mean it was negligent on the part of the city, not Mr. Holligan, of course," the lawyer said. "I think the city should not go unpunished for such negligence."

"Oh, I see what you mean," said Tim. "I'll try and find him in a day or two."

Tim found him, and they sat in a booth together, the three of them—the lawyer, Tim, and The Slugger.

"It was pure negligence," said the lawyer.

"I wasn't doing anybody any harm," said The Slugger. "I was walking along and I bunked into this here thing and down I went—"

"Shut up, Slugger. Let the lawyer talk," said Tim.

"I have seldom heard of a case of more obvious negligence," the lawyer continued. "A stormy night, a citizen on his way home, and the grating sticking up as a menace to each and every taxpayer. The most reprehensible thing I've ever heard of. Have you any money saved up, Mr. Holligan?"

"Who, me?" said The Slugger.

"Shut up, Slugger," Tim said. "What size of money are you talking about, sir?"

"I was trying to estimate if Mr. Holligan could stand the cost of a lawsuit, in the event it would be unsuccessful, but I don't see how it could be when the negligence is so apparent," the lawyer said.

"Mr. Holligan is a workingman," Tim said, "and with the cost of living what it is today, he hasn't been able to set much aside."

"And by this broken leg this honest workingman has been deprived of a chance of a livelihood all these months," the lawyer chimed in.

"It hurts worse in the damp weather," The Slugger said.

"Shut up, Slugger. Let me handle this," said Tim. "Now, is there any way you could treat this on a contingency base? I heard there was times a lawyer would take a cut of what he gets for the man he's speaking up for, and let that be his end of the deal. Could we work it out that way for the Slug—I mean Mr. Holligan?"

"The Bar Association does not approve of such arrangements," the lawyer said.

"But Mr. Holligan doesn't happen to have any money at this time," Tim said.

"It is possible that Mr. Holligan may come into some money, however," said the lawyer. "In which event he would be readily able to meet my fee."

"That is possible," said Tim. "Keep quiet, Slugger."

"We shall proceed on that basis," the lawyer declared. "I am suing for thirty thousand dollars for gross negligence. Carroll M. Holligan versus the City of New York."

"He has my real name, Tim," said The Slugger. "Can you beat that, the way these fellows get to know things. My real name, Carroll M. Holligan!"

"All right, Slugger, go up to Jimmy there at the bar, and tell him I told you to have a drink," said Tim.

"Thanks, Tim. Thank you very much," said The Slugger. "Glad to meet you, sir." This last was to the lawyer. He went out of the booth on his cane and bad leg, and started over to the bar, glancing back at Tim as he did so. Tim signaled O.K. to Jimmy the barkeep. The Slugger, by no means as dumb as he seems, walked proudly forward and asked for rye-and-water—plain water, if you please. "They're going to get me thirty thousand dollars for me broken leg," he said. "I'll square this drink up with you when I get it. And it's many a drink you'll have on me after that. You're a good boy, Jimmy, and don't think I won't take care of you after I get my money. I'm not the kind that forgets his friends, Jimmy, God bless you."

The Slugger was on the way to being a made man.

It came to be May and everything lovely along the avenue. Especially with The Slugger. The kids were singing on the stoops at evening, usually singing "Just Around the Corner There's a Bluebird on High." There wasn't a bluebird within eight miles of the stoops they were on, but that made no difference. The Slugger was a man of substance then. He was a thirty-thousand-dollar man, because his case was "pending," as they say. What did he show up in on fine sun-shiny days but white shoes and white flannel pants and a blue coat, with a starched white shirt beneath the coat and a good straw hat on top of it all. He was still walking with a cane. He got the white flannels from a little store that had them left over from years ago. The proprietor had heard about The Slugger's thirty thousand dollars, which he hadn't got yet, and so the proprietor trusted him.

Down would come The Slugger, limping on his cane, and he would stand for a minute, using the cane to beat time for the children singing on the stoop:

> "Just erround a corner
> They's a blooboid on high . . . "

They would sing, and The Slugger would move his cane back and forth in the air. It was beautiful to see. Then he'd go away, on the route to the nearest saloon.

The Slugger was a happy man, with the phantom figure "$30,000" dancing always in the back of his head like a tiny, tiny Bill Robinson tapping out an endless jolly tune with his feet, the way Bill used to do. He had credit everywhere. He'd walk in, have a rye-and-plain-water, and they'd all say, the men behind the bar, "That's all right, Slugger, don't worry about it."

"Mark it down," he'd say with a grand air, and ask whoever was next to him to have a drink. They would.

"Goodbye, Jimmy [or Joe, or Ed]," The Slugger would say. He'd go out then, in the twilight of the avenue, and feel very good.

So would the bartender he left behind. The bartender would swab a glass under the bar, washing it out, and then he would find some pal in front of the bar and say to him, "The old Slugger. Awful nice little feller. I always liked him. He got thirty thousand dollars coming, they tell me, from that time he hurt his leg. He got it broke. He says it pains him something terrible in wet weather. Even damp weather. It's lovely out today."

The lawyer told The Slugger not to throw away the cane even if he felt he didn't need it any more. Some days he didn't need it, but he forgot the idea the lawyer had, which was to keep him on a cane until the case came up in court. So some fine days The Slugger, with a few jolts in him bought out of his merciless amount of credit here and there, would be walking around spry as anyone could be, with the cane under his arm.

"The lawyer told me never go out without the cane," he'd say. "Here it is. I never go out without it. A day like this, it doesn't pain me at all."

Tim was there, as a bystander, when The Slugger made his appearance in the court. He said it was magnificent, no less a word would do for it, magnificent. It was a damp day, as luck would have it. The Slugger's leg really pained him.

"They called him over to the witness chair," Tim said that night. "He came down the aisle leaning on the cane, and I almost felt like getting up and helping him myself. He seemed to be struggling to get to the witness chair. That's the one to the left of the judge and in front of the jury box. It was magnificent."

"What was?" Jake asked him. He was one of the men listening that night to Tim. "What was?"

"The way The Slugger came down the aisle and sat in the witness chair," said Tim. "And the only answer I remember. The lawyer asked him—and I remember this next part clearly—he asked him, 'What happened, Mr. Holligan?' And The Slugger sat there and answered him, 'I was trying to go home and this grating stuck up and I fell down and broke my poor leg.' The way he said it, you would think that the leg was not a part of him but a friend that he did not want any misfortune to fall to. 'I broke my poor leg,' he said. The lawyer—a very smart man, I believe—said, 'That's all, Mr. Holligan.' I don't remember what followed. It was magnificent."

"It was," Jake said.

It wound up that The Slugger got eleven thousand dollars. That is, the jury awarded him that. The lawyer took three thousand. That left The Slugger eight thousand. He owed $47.60 at Morley's. He owed $83.50 at Colcannon's. He owed the man for the white flannels and the blue coat and the straw hat. He owed everybody. The happy time was over. But not eternally. Because Tim took charge then.

"Will you give me the power of attorney?" Tim asked him.

"You got the power of anything," The Slugger said. "I never met a more powerful man."

Then Tim had the lawyer turn over to him what was left of The Slugger's money, and he will give it out to him twenty-five or thirty dollars a week as long as it lasts. Probably a little bit longer. Tim is that kind of man.

Even if it's Mexico nothing flashy ever happens to Grogan

Grogan the Horseplayer vanished out of this neighborhood nearly two years ago and he showed up quietly again, the way he does everything, about two weeks ago. It turned out nothing had happened to him except he been in Mexico a couple of years nearly. All he had for the two years was a bishop's ring with a cross into the design of it. It was what they call a topaz and explaining about the ring is how Grogan told about Mexico and how it was there.

Nothing big ever happens to Grogan because he is a quiet little man now past fifty with glasses and all he wants is that nobody bother him so that he can just go along betting on horses, studying them out and maybe win a few dollars now and then. He isn't the kind that talks about having big adventures for the simple reason he don't have them whether it is in Mexico or on Third Avenue. Just the same, when Tim that owns this saloon asked him about the ring, what Grogan told him turned out to be a story that passed an hour away for two or three regulars standing with Tim at the end of the bar.

"Did you eat all right while you were down there in Mexico?" Tim asked him. The uncertain way Grogan the Horseplayer lives he sometimes doesn't eat.

"Sometimes I et all right," Grogan said, the solemn way he talks, looking over the tops of his glasses.

"Would you say most of the time you did?" Tim asked him then, because you have to pull things out of Grogan, he's not much of a self-starter to tell about anything.

"After a while I did," Grogan said. "There was a young woman there, her family and her sold a kind of sangwiches, Mexican sangwiches they call *tacos*. This young woman didn't have anybody to be with, and so I after a while et the sangwiches. I mean her family and me got to be friends and this young woman, her name was Carmela, we got to be friends, it's how I got that bishop's ring I showed you the first day I got home."

If you knew Grogan that would sound strange a little, because Grogan is a kind of uncle guy, never heard of him in connection with any young woman or even his own age woman. You can't have it pointed out too often about Grogan it's practically only horses he cares about at all. Women are out of it entirely. You'd know that if you knew Grogan.

Grogan got into Mexico a way you wouldn't think of right off. He got respectable cousins lives in Bridgeport, they're the very opposite of him. They work hard all the time and save up money and then they go traveling, at least they used to before all the trouble with gasoline and autos. And some-how they like Grogan. Every old guy like that seems to have somebody for relatives somewhere who like him, even if millions of other people in a city like this pays no attention to him. So the way Grogan vanished from the neighbor-hood was that these cousins came to town and said to Gro-gan they were going to drive to Mexico to see the place and he could come with them if he wanted. He went with them and what happen was that after they got to Mexico Grogan got tired of the relatives, and anyway he lost his citizenship papers and couldn't get out very handy. The result was the relatives came home without him, and there was Grogan the Horseplayer in Mexico City. It made no difference to him, because wherever he is, he always falls in with people in his quiet way.

"This place where this Mexican family sold the sang-wiches was a nice place to go at night, the way you'd go to Bickford's and have something to eat late at night if you were around here," Grogan said. "They also had cornflakes, and lots of Mexican restaurants never heard of cornflakes. So I fell into the habit going there every night and eating cornflakes and reading the papers."

Like nearly all the horseplayers there are, Grogan got what they call an ace in the hole. That is, a way to get some money always. You run out of money betting on horses eventually and the ace in the hole is the way you can get a stake again. With Grogan this is painting signs and doing lettering. He can do that very well, can even draw a decoration picture on the signs if wanted. He fell in with a sign-painting Mexican had a studio down there, and he got a few pesos out of that, and that's how he had enough to go into this place for the cornflakes every night.

"They were a nice family that run this place," Grogan said. "The mother had two daughters, one was Carmela and the other was Maria. They worked hard and they kept the place clean. Lots of the Mexican restaurants ain't, but this one was. Clean, I mean. It showed that they were a good family and they were proud of how clean it was. I got able to talk to them a little after a while, a Spanish word here, Spanish word there, and they liked to be as American as they could.

"A thing that showed how they liked to be American was that they saved up what they made in this restaurant and they put an American bathroom into their house. It don't seem much here, but an American bathroom is a hell of a big thing in a Mexican house. It shows how good you're getting along. Like people here would get along pretty good and first thing they might do is buy a piano like a Steinway, only among these Mexican people it wouldn't be a Steinway piano, it would be an American bathroom they would have put in. This family had an American bathroom.

"They asked me to their house after the night I took this

Carmela to a dance. I would never ast her, but her mother come over to my table in the restaurant and in some words of English, some of Spanish, she ast me would I take Carmela to a dance. I was surprised because a Mexican mother is very careful like that, and it was a hell of a compliment she would ask me that. I didn't have much money that night, but the mother explained she had the tickets, and I took Carmela to the dance. We got along fine, and at the dance I learned a great song. It is a song that says that 'Guadalajara Will Never Back Down.' That Guadalajara is a place outside Mexico City that's got a lot of pride about itself.

"Anyway, after I took this young woman to the dance, they ast me to their house and it was very nice there. I was living in a joint, pretty disappointing place to live if you're an American. And so it was nice to go out to the Mexicans' house and sit there at night. The whole family would be there after the restaurant close up. I could sit there and read about the bullfights, which are quite a thing down there. It was tough going on the reading, because these papers got printed in Spanish. I tried to prowl a little Spanish into my head talking to this one and that one, and did good enough at it. But reading the bullfight sheets was harder than the plain talking-Spanish they got, so reading was a hell of a job. It was easier picking the winner at the bullfights than out of the racing papers, though. Pradickly always the same winner at the bullfights, the guy with the sword. The bull only win once in a dog's age. But anyway, later on they got a racetrack opened up and made the whole city seem more homelike. They call it the Hipodromo of the Americas, in Spanish it is *de las Americas*. With that opened up I could go back to horses and doping them out. It was certainly fine sitting in this Mexican house with the race dope at night and these people were very happy around the house and so was I, too. They were tickled to death when I finely got up enough courage and ast them could I take a bath in their American bathroom, and after that I took baths there regularly, and it was a God's blessing for me. We used to sit there at night and the house was warm and comfortable and they would ask about New York and Carmela would make me coffee and I would tell them about New York. They didn't believe half of it, and Carmela would say, 'Don't tell any more lies, please, Señor Grogahn, go back to your *caballos*.' That's horses in Spanish.

"There was one thing sad about Carmela that I found out," Grogan said. "She was very dark, and her sister would kid her in Spanish about it when they had a little quarrel about nothing. Her sister would say *'Obscoora!'* That means dark and Carmela would look embarrassed and quick look over at me when her sister said it. She was wondering did I know what it meant, but I would keep on reading the racing paper. I never let on. Anyway, being dark really made this Carmela prettier, maybe not the way women are pretty up here in New York. But this Carmela look like a pretty Buddha statue, small and her face round and wide like a carved-out Buddha statue made from a dark wood of some kind.

"That's the way it would be in this Mexican house, and I guess everybody got vanity, because I remember how for once in my life I felt like a big shot. That was because *I* was so welcome there and these nice Mexicans didn't know hardly anybody knew me in New York. They thought I was a big New York American, not that I lied or anything. I didn't, they just naturally made me welcome because they were people that's not complicated at all and to them maybe a New Yorker was really something, even a horseplayer.

"But you got to come home sometimes, if where you belong is here, and finely I got to thinking how it would be back on Third Avenue. They felt bad when I told them I was going. I got the citizenship-papers thing fixed up, and with all the documents coming to me that I filled out at their house, they thought all the more I was a somebody. That wasn't why they were so good. They were just what you call kind people anyway, and they cried when I was going. The mother, her name was Rosaria, she cried too. I couldn't believe it. Then when I was going, Carmela, in front her mother and sister, gave me the bishop's ring. It seems a Mexican one time kept eating in the restaurant for quite a while on the cuff, and they let him because they kind of knew him. He couldn't pay and so one day he gave them this ring, no questions ast. They wouldn't do anything with the ring because it looked you might say holy to them. They are very religious people, most of them down there, or else they hate religion entirely. This family was the very religious kind. So instead cashing in the ring, they had kept holding onto it, until the night I was going and Carmela said to me, 'I would like Señor Grogahn to have this ring, my mother would too. It is a farewell, to let you know always there will be a corner in this *casa* if you ever come back to read your paper about the *caballos*. And if you are without money sometime for a *caballo*, it is all right to sell this ring, we know it could happen you'd have to have money for that.' This Carmela said this in Spanish slow, and her mother stood there and I had to take the ring and go away.

"That's all there is about the ring," Grogan said. "I can get it sometime again, if I run into a good streak."

"Is it gone?" Tim asked him.

"I wouldn't say it is gone," Grogan said. "I was broke and I owed the bookie forty-eight dollars a couple days after I got home. He gimme sixty dollars on the ring. He said he would not sell this bishop's ring and I could get it back if I maybe caught a couple winners and got some dough. I think that would be all right with this young woman Carmela. She was all right. I liked her very much, but of course I never told her I did. I mean I never told her I liked her."

Bartender here takes dislike to "Deep in the Heart of Texas"

Paddy Ferrarty, the night bartender in this place on Third Avenue, lives in a furnished room. It's run by a landlady by the name Miss Myers. Paddy's single. He sleeps daytimes and reads Westerns. Everybody in furnished rooms reads Westerns and in furnished-room places there's always a pile of Westerns in the basement if your own runs out; that is, you've got it all read through.

That doesn't have much to do with what Paddy did a little while ago, except that he really likes the Old West from reading so much Westerns, even if he has never been out of New York since he landed from Ireland.

"I don't know why a furnished room gets lonesome at five o'clock nearly on the dot every day," Paddy was saying the other night, when hardly anybody was in the gin mill. "I don't like work—it's the curse of the world—but damn if I don't almost want to get to work out of the furnished room about five o'clock.

"Every day when it happens that way I begin going to work and I hope every day the joint will be livelier than home, where I'm sick of. But the same time I hope it won't get too lively with people hollering or maybe some guy reciting. Reciters are one of the terrors of tending bar. So are people striking up friendships with strangers at the bar that always ends in fights. And now they got juke boxes.

"Juke boxes are the curse of the world. They got me nuts and they got every other bartender nuts, especially a bartender that works nights.

"They first began to get me cuckoo when they had on ours 'El Rancho Reeyo Grandy.' It had a part where drunks hollered, just the same as this 'Heart of Texas' got a place drunks got to clap.

"I just thought I'd go nuts with the Reeyo Grandy one but I was sure of it with this 'The prairie sky is wide and high,' and then the goddam four claps.

"Or is it three claps? One of the things that drives you crazy is that. Some gives three claps and some gives four and they're all clapping together at the bar. Only they're not clapping together. How can they, some giving three claps and some giving four?

"One guy I see put in eighteen nickels one after the other, all for the 'Heart of Texas.' He got a beer, give me a dollar, and wanted all-nickels change, which I gave him, and one by one in they went till I nearly jump over the bar.

"The hell of it is there's good tunes on there, too, and I wouldn't want it said I'm a guy hates music's guts. They got one on there a meddalee of Stross waltzes. It's Number 15. I use to be one of the best waltzers there was, only my feet are all stove down now from floors behind bars that got no give to them, like walking on cement. They're killing me right now, my feet, on top of getting mad about the 'Heart of Texas.' Thank God I got rid of that record.

"The way I got rid of it—well, I had to get tough. First I was going to ask the boss would he for God's sake jimmy that record out of there, but the boss is the boss, good enough in his way but stubborn about the customers wants this and the customers wants that. A man can't devote his life to the customers, but what sense telling that to the boss? Anyway, I figure the fox is his own best messenger, they used to say back home in Maynooth, and the next afternoon I came in myself to the gin mill about two o'clock.

"That was a Tuesday, the day the guy comes around to empty the juke box and once in a while he puts in new records.

" 'Get the "Heart of Texas" the hell out of there,' I said to him when he got the front of the machine down. The boss wasn't there, lucky enough. 'You ain't running the joint and it takes in a lot of nickels,' the juke-box guy said. 'All right, it takes in a lot of nickels and it's driving me nuts,' I told him. 'Out comes the "Heart of Texas" or I'll cut the wire. I'll sabotize the whole goddam thing, job or no job.' 'I'm telling you it takes in a lot of nickels and he got to have the nickels to pay for the ice machine,' the guy said.

"I forgot to tell about how they get you hemmed in if you run a gin mill. They sell you an ice machine for the bar—costs about twenty-three hundred dollars, imagine that—and you pay for it by dropping five quarters in a slot every day at the end of the bar. Like an old gas meter. So the money out of the juke box goes into quarters to put into the ice-machine slot. The way I figure it that leaves everybody where he was, only with two machines he didn't want in the first place.

" 'Get the "Heart of Texas" the hell out of there,' I told him, 'or, bejeezus, I'll screw up the icebox too.' Well, there was some more words. No fist fight, nothing.

"Sum and substance is he took it out and put in a good one. Number 17. 'Hin*doo*stan.' It's got a part at the end where a bass fiddle got a nice lilt to it. And jeez, do I get many a good peace of mind when some dame will be standing at the bar and yell to a guy, 'Hey, Eddie, put on "Heart of Texas." ' I don't say anything. I just think how she'll play hell getting the 'Heart of Texas' in here."

Don't scrub off these names

If a wife could be as patient as Grogan the Horseplayer's landlady, there would be hardly any old guys living alone in furnished rooms the way there are hundreds of them now. One time Grogan owed his landlady ninety weeks' rent. That will give you some idea about Grogan's landlady. She got more tolerance than you can shake a stick at and she certainly is a fine woman. She's an elderly woman, seems to understand horseplayers and not be bothered by them as much as other people are.

This rooming house where Grogan lives is quite a place once you get to understand it. It is an old brownstone house, once upon a time worth forty thousand dollars. That part of it comes in to what happened with Grogan, how much the house was worth and all. You wouldn't notice this house among thousands of houses like it in different parts of Manhattan. It's just a four-story affair, with a stoop, and a gate door under the stoop, the kind of door you used to go through into hundreds of speakeasies in the old days.

Grogan's rent got piled up to ninety weeks that time because he's the kind of old guy you trust once you get to know him. He is quiet and more than fifty and wears glasses. He clears his throat before he talks, and when he does talk it is mostly about racehorses. A gin-mill man that knows Grogan for years said one time about him, "Grogan is so goddam honest he don't *have* to pay you." What he meant was that there are a lot of guys, if they borrow five bucks, let's say, why two minutes afterward you begin worrying are they going to cheat you out of it and never pay you back. But with Grogan, if he borrows anything and a couple months goes by, even a couple years, you still got confidence that as soon as he can get around to it Grogan will pay you back.

That accounts partly for Mrs. Benoit, that's Grogan the Horseplayer's landlady, letting the rent run up to ninety weeks. In money it was two hundred and seventy dollars, because he has a rent of only three bucks a week. That's all out of kilter with rents now, but Mrs. Benoit decided years ago that Grogan's rent was three bucks a week and it never changed. Anyway, Grogan just kept putting it off week after week, sometimes being in the hole on account of horses, sometimes having to buy some shoes or something, and there was never enough left for the rent, so what he owed piled up. Never once did Mrs. Benoit bother him. She knew Grogan would pay up sometime. Then he went to Mexico. Some cousins took him, and he was gone a year and a half, and back he comes, walking into the rooming house and saying "Hello, Mrs. Benoit," after he cleared his throat. And he paid her sixty bucks on the two-seventy. He got the sixty bucks selling a bishop's ring that a Mexican family gave him for a goodbye gift when he left Mexico City. They were very fond of him.

Grogan's got an ace in the hole to keep up to, or at least not too far behind, the horses. He is a crackerjack commercial artist, drawing pictures of hams and bacons and, at Thanksgiving, Puritan girls carrying in turkeys, for the ad agencies, but he usually works at it only to get money for horses. Well, he had a fit of working as hard as you could imagine right after he came back from Mexico and he paid off the two-ten. It was working money, earned from working, not from horses, and how Grogan paid the landlady with it so steady was a surprise to those that know him and realize he'd rather put every cent on horses than do anything else with money. Here's how he did it.

In the afternoons, Grogan would sit around in Mrs. Benoit's basement apartment calling bets on the phone to a puny kind of bookie. The bookie is a Greek runs a flower store, but he watches the entries and results more than he cares a damn about the rhododendrons.

These afternoons would show you how patient Mrs. Benoit is. With Grogan studying the *Racing Form,* then telephoning to the Greek every couple of minutes, and the radio going steadily all the time, it would make anybody jumpy, but not Mrs. Benoit. She would stand there ironing perhaps, just pushing the iron back and forth and now and then reaching for something else out of the clothesbasket, while Grogan rushed to the telephone or turned the radio up louder so he wouldn't miss a result coming in.

This basement apartment is Mrs. Benoit's own, and it is the only one with a telephone in the house. Grogan and the others got an arrangement they leave a nickel down on a plate by the phone every time they use it, so as not to cost Mrs. Benoit anything for horse calls or any other kind. To her it must be a nuisance, but away back she is a woman of French descent and she does not seem to get mad at the things that Americans get mad at. That is, she does not get mad at people being peculiar, but seems to figure everyone has his own way of being and there's no sense trying to change it.

For example, over the telephone in her apartment, written on the wall, it says this:

Don't Scrub Off
These Names

And underneath that are some names written out very plain. They need to be explained. These names are there because one of the guys who lives in the house is Clancy. You might call him an Irish gigolo. That's the way he gets along without working, he preys on women. But it is only fair to say he doesn't hurt them any. They are all elderly women that Clancy makes a point of striking up an acquaintance with in cocktail bars.

Clancy is a terrible fake of a guy, but in a way harmless. He plays up this "Dublin Irish" stuff and can talk pretty fancy in a Dublin way. He wears shirts that have high soft collars, with tabs in them, they call them tab collars. They're the kind of collars Englishmen wear, and they give Clancy a high-brow kind of look. He borrows suits from nearly everybody in the house. It's a remarkable thing, but everybody's clothes seem to fit Clancy and he is a very persuasive talker, can talk everybody into lending him suits, so much so that often he gets to borrow a new suit before the guy who owns it has it on twice himself.

Anyway, Clancy looks good dolled up, and he talks fine, and his regular routine is meeting these lonesome old ladies in the cocktail lounges and shining up to them. First thing you know, they're having him to dinner at their apartment, and he talks about money coming from the old country, and after a couple of dinners he tells them his money didn't come and he is hard pressed, and he borrows fifty or a hundred. That's boiling it down pretty much, how Clancy works, but that's the guts of it. He's such a faker he lies about nearly everything, more or less to keep in practice, and to each new old lady he gives a different name. He gives names he thinks are fancy, and they're so much so they're almost silly. But silly or not, he comes back and writes the latest name down on the telephone list on the wall. The idea is, known to everybody in the house and above all to Mrs. Benoit, that when there's a telephone call for a strange name, why you look at the list and if the name is there you say, "Yes, he's home. Just a moment, please, I'll call him." Then you holler for Clancy, being sure to keep a hand over the transmitter, because you know that Clancy has given this name to one of his old rich ladies. Five of the names that were written on the wall all together lately were these:

> Mr. Cavendish
> Mr. Lancet
> Mr. Morency
> Mr. De Courcey
> Mr. Baltimore

That Mrs. Benoit puts up with such nonsense as Clancy and his names is another instance what a patient woman she is. To say nothing of Mallan. He's another one lives in the house, and he's an out-and-out drunk. Like all the others except Clancy, this Mallan is past fifty, and he's still getting drunk somehow every night, until he has a rum blossom for a nose and purple veins on his grinny face.

What would make Mallan annoying anywhere but at Mrs. Benoit's is the habit he has of getting a *Daily News* when the bars close up at 4 A.M. He gets a *Daily News* without fail, reads it as best he can, although drunk, in a

Shanty near the rooming house. Then at half past four in the morning, in he goes to the house, stomps up the stairs, and wakes up Grogan, then Clancy and a couple other inmates, one after the other.

"Come on, sit up!" he always says. "Sit up and take the Intelligence Test! Wake up and take the Intelligence Test!"

And then he reads out the questions in the Intelligence Test, loud, and shaking Grogan, or whoever it is, while he reads off the questions, that are always something like this: "Astigmatism refers to a disorder of which organ?" Then Mallan will continue to read, loud and slow, the list of organs, while Grogan blinks in bed:

"Liver? . . . Ear? . . . Heart? . . . Eye?"

And Grogan, or whoever it is, will want to get it over with and get Mallan out of the room, so he'll say "Eye!" if he knows that's the answer.

"Right!" Mallan will holler. Then he'll go on to the next question, which might be this: "A statue inscribed MCCCC-XCII would probably represent Julius Caesar, Columbus, Washington, or Lincoln?"

It turns out to be, in this instance, Columbus, but hardly anybody could wake up and answer one like that. Just the same, Mallan teeters on the edge of the bed until Grogan gets the right answer, and then he hollers "Right!" And after Mallan has given the Intelligence Test to Grogan and

Clancy and maybe a couple of others, why he staggers to bed himself, and that's that. He's gone through that rigamarole hundreds of times, and it goes to show you how much patience Mrs. Benoit has to let a guy like that keep on living in the house.

Well, to get back to Grogan, and the afternoons down in the basement apartment, betting the horses while Mrs. Benoit does her ironing. Grogan used to run completely out of money doing that. But somehow, when he came back from Mexico and started paying up the remaining two hundred and ten dollars after he paid the ring money, why he cut down on betting, until gradually it was mostly mind bets. He'd pick horses but not call the Greek, and he'd listen to results. Sometimes he'd be furious he didn't bet one that turned out to be a winner. More often he'd be tickled to death he didn't bet, because it was a loser. "I save two bucks on that one," Grogan would say. And to make a game out of it, why he'd hand Mrs. Benoit the two bucks and say, "Take that off what I owe you, will you please, Mrs. Benoit?"

"Yes, Mr. Grogan," Mrs. Benoit would say, putting down the flatiron, or whatever she was using at the moment. "Thank you. I'll mark it down."

Well, in only a couple of months, Grogan was in the clear on the ninety weeks' rent. And the funny thing was, he kept right on going on with the same scheme after he got the rent paid off. In a few more weeks, he had nearly a hundred and fifty "on deposit," you might say, with Mrs. Benoit. She never said a word to egg him on, except in her own way, perhaps, of remarking, "That's very good, Mr. Grogan. You have fifty-six dollars"—or whatever it was—"now. I'll mind it for you."

Grogan acted as if this was the first time, and him past fifty years of age, that he ever heard of saving money. He got fascinated by the idea and when the money Mrs. Benoit had for him got up to three hundred and sixty, he told her one day what was in his head. He cleared his throat, the way he always does, and he said, "That's a great spot, that Mexico, Mrs. Benoit. And I'm going to go back down there, only this time with dough. For a little while, I can be a rich American. It'll certainly be something, walking in on that Mexican family I know. They were swell to me when I was down there broke, and here I'll come walking in to them, take them to the bullfights, the best seats, not out in what they call the *sol*. That's the sun seats, you know, what we call at a ball game the bleachers. And I can buy them stuff knock their eye out. When I get a thousand bucks, just a little more than a thousand, so I can get there at the Mexican house with the whole even thousand after my fare, why off I go to Mexico!"

That was quite a speech for Grogan, but he was hopped up with the idea. He told his plan later to Clancy. Fake or no fake, Clancy was a guy Grogan liked, and he told him stuff like that.

It's funny, too, in a place like Mrs. Benoit's, that even accidents works out good. You could take for example about the chimney. What happened about the chimney was that it gave out too much smoke. O.K., only nearly next door is a hotel, higher than Mrs. Benoit's place. And when the wind blew right, the smoke went into some of the hotel rooms. The guests kicked and wouldn't stay there and it was a ticklesome situation. Problem was, you couldn't deny the rooming house had to have heat—that's human. And there's laws against smoke, but they're tricky laws, and it wasn't too much smoke legally, you might say, and so here was a hell of a situation, an accident, too, the whole of it, not planned by anybody, but the situation worked out good. The hotel men tried to bully Mrs. Benoit first, but she wouldn't scare. So the upshot was that the hotel men came to Mrs. Benoit and they put up this proposition: "Say we hook up the heat from the hotel into your place, will you shut off your furnace, Mrs. Benoit?" That would be O.K., she said, and no sooner said than done. So the accident of the smoke saved Mrs. Benoit the coal money, to say nothing saving the trouble running the furnace. There never was a time when she didn't have to skimp to run the place. The finances of it was that when Mrs. Benoit's husband died years ago he left her money and she bought the house with it. It was supposed then to be worth forty thousand, but nowadays, why nothing like forty thousand. And the mortgage, even lately, was only down to nineteen thousand dollars. You couldn't get that for the house if you wanted to sell it, is what Mrs. Benoit said.

She said that one afternoon only lately. Grogan had shut off the radio because the races were over and the announcer had slumped into talking about Warsaw and Pisa. Clancy was blathering his way through making some tea. While he made it on a little stove in Mrs. Benoit's apartment, he said for the thousandth time in a year, "I have this tea sent to me specially from Boston."

And Mrs. Benoit said in her soft voice, "I know you do, Mr. Clancy. It's very nice." She knew and Grogan knew, sitting there, you could get the same tea anywhere, but Clancy went to great trouble to have it sent from Boston anyway.

Well, after that, Clancy poured out the tea, talking in big words all the while, and Mrs. Benoit went on talking about the house. "The bank told me a funny thing. I couldn't believe it," she said. "It didn't sound like something a bank would say."

Grogan cleared his throat. He'd been talking about Mexico again and he thought he was talking too much about it, although he was going there soon and it was all he could think of. "What did the bank say?" he asked, after a swig of the tea.

"They said that if I put up two thousand dollars, they'd cut the mortgage down to twelve thousand dollars, instead of it being nineteen thousand dollars the way it is now. Does that sound like a bank?"

"The financial situation in these times is extremely unorthodox," said Clancy, swinging into the big words, as usual.

Grogan cleared his throat again. "Do I get it right? They said if you put up two thousand dollars, they'd cut it down by seven thousand?" he asked.

"That's it," Mrs. Benoit said. "If I put up the two thousand, which I can't because I only scraped together a thousand dollars in all these years—well, if I put up the two, then they'd take off seven thousand off my shoulders. Then the interest would be a lot less and I could really make a little money on this house."

"Seven thousand for two thousand," Grogan said. He put down his cup and meandered out the door to the stairway. "Excuse me," he said over the banister as he went up to his room.

Clancy told about it later. He said Grogan come down again in a few minutes.

"I kept track upstairs in a book," he said to Mrs. Benoit. "Is it a thousand and seventy, exactly, that I got for Mexico?"

"It's more than a thousand, I know," said Mrs. Benoit. "Without looking in my book, I know that."

Grogan stared her in the eye, Clancy said, and then he says, "Look, Mrs. Benoit. I don't have to go to Mexico yet. You take my thousand and your thousand and give it to the bank. Look! I don't want a lot of talk and guff about it. Give them the two thousand quick and get credit for seven thousand. Seven to two on a mortgage! Jeez!"

"Oh, no, Mr. Grogan!" Mrs. Benoit said, and she turned pale. "It's for Mexico."

"Look," Grogan said, mad. "I don't want any guff about it. I never had a thousand bucks before and I don't know that I like it. It makes me nervous. It don't feel like me. Mexico will be better next year. Clancy, come on to the delicatessen with me."

And out they went, Clancy and Grogan. The way Clancy told it later, after the whole thing got straightened out and the mortgage cut down to twelve thousand, he got Grogan sore on the sidewalk outside the delicatessen. He did it ribbing him. Clancy said to him, "You chump, you couldn't resist the price, that's what happened to you. Once you heard it was seven to two on a mortgage, and a bank the sucker into the bargain, why you couldn't resist it!"

Grogan burned up. "No such thing," he growled at Clancy. "It's a question of a room. How many years is three hundred and thirty-three and a third weeks? That's how long I got a room paid up. It's a matter of a room. No seven-to-two stuff or what they call sentiment. Just cold-turkey business, you lousy faker!"

They'd have taken him if he was only a torso

The war got a lot of twists to it, but one good thing was the way it dubbed up the Man in the Green Overcoat.

He's a man doesn't mean any harm at the bottom of anything he does, but he certainly got a great weakness for making hard-and-fast decisions for other people. Around this gin mill on Third Avenue they put up with him for some reason, and people even listen to him and pay attention, although they ought to know better by this time.

The Man in the Green Overcoat's past fifty and that's been the matter with him his whole life, those decisions he's always making. All the decisions are for somebody else. If somebody around there gets up to the point he got to make a decision one way or the other, the Man in the Green Overcoat is sure as hell to step up and make the decision for him. About half the things he says begins with the words, "If I was you, I tell you what I'd do." No difference at all what it is, whether it's a horse to bet on or not, or whether it's somebody wondering should they get married or not. Bing! This man horns in on the situation somehow and decides for the guy. He gets talking to him and mentally like gives him a push and settles the matter with advice. Horse or wedding, the advice turns out wrong.

Funny they'd listen to him, so much of his fixing turned sour year after year. But he's got a very persuading way about him, and there you are. People do listen. It's been going on for years around this saloon. Tim, that owns the place, has seen many an instance of it.

That's the point of it, how Tim knew so well about this guy and how he was proud of fixing things up without seeming to realize they turn out bad nine times out of ten. They call him the Man in the Green Overcoat, never give him any other name even if that's a long name, because in winter he always wore a terrible green overcoat. Every winter.

Anyway, there's a medium-young regular customer comes in this saloon, and if ever a man wanted down in his heart to get into the Army this regular did. His name was Marty. Well, it wasn't altogether to be patriotic that he was nuts to get into the Army. Thousands of other guys breaking their necks, you might say, to keep out of it, but there was a girl mixed into Marty's case. He was stuck on her. Seem she like him well enough, but not too hot about him, let's say.

Well, Marty would come in this place time and time again, and he'd have a few slugs and get talking to Tim and cry-babying about this girl. And he'd cry-baby because they passed him up for the Army. That was quite a while ago, when it was tough to get in for some. Hard to realize that now, but there was such a time.

Marty was one of those cases where his feet was only pretty good. And his eyes was only pretty good, and his ears was only pretty good and the same with his lungs. Nothing stand out real good all over him. And his heart was even a little less than pretty good, they said. They said it had a habit of stopping and starting unexplained for a second or two, something like a bum electric icebox. He wasn't a cripple any part, but the sum-up of only being pretty good all over wound up with the doctors calling no dice on him. They don't want him. He looks to them like a pension case before he'd even get the soldier suit on.

To get to what happen, you got to hear about this night a few months ago, along about ten o'clock at night. Hardly anybody was in the saloon, and Tim was behind the bar having a cup of tea. First Marty come in and after he knocked over a couple of slugs, why he begin talking confidential to Tim, and of course soon cry-babying about the girl.

Not to go into the thing too much, Marty got the idea this girl is too good for him, that's the guts of it. Then he says to Tim, "Tim, I see a picture in the paper it was Winthrop Rockefeller and a couple other soldiers lined up for their picture. He's a Rockefeller that's in the Army. This was quite a while ago, but the picture stuck in my mind. These other soldiers was Di Salvos or Kellys, just neighborhood boys, and what hit me between the eyes, they all looked like Winthrop Rockefeller. Or maybe he looked like them."

Marty went on talking, Tim listening, and Marty says, "That uniform moves Winthrop Rockefeller down a little, it seem to me, and it moves these other fellers up a little. It evens things up. It'd move me up a little if I could get into one of those uniforms. They're calling me in tomorrer, the draft board, but they'll turn me down, I'm afraid."

Course Tim knew what Marty was driving at. It's that it would boost him a peg with the girl if he would get into the Army. Tim knows the girl, a neighborhood kid grew up around here, a nice kid all right, her name is Eileen Callan.

Well, after that talk out goes Marty finally, still broodin' around. There's nobody in the place for a while but Tim, and then in comes, of all people, old Mr. Masafin. He hadn't been in the place for months. He don't work any more, he's retired, a fine old man, ran two grocery stores for forty years, always around here and knew everybody since they were kids and their fathers before them.

Old Mr. Masafin orders a Jameson, they still got a little of that put away for special customers. Tim ask him why he been ducking the place, ask him in a nice way, of course. He hadn't been in there for months.

"I haven't been any place for months," says Mr. Masafin, sore. "I'm half afraid to go any place. You know I'm on the draft board, and by God everybody I meet, if I have a drink anywhere or go to play cards anywhere, it winds up somebody tries to put the fix in to keep somebody out of the Army.

"It's sickening," he says. "We're trying to do this job fair and square and we've been doing it fair and square. It's the most thankless job in the whole war. We work on the draft board for free and we don't get a uniform, or a title even, the way they do in Washington. We just work in some schoolroom turned over to us and it smells of chalk powder off the blackboards and sweaty kids. What the hell thanks do we get?"

The old man have another Jameson and Tim some tea and old Masafin goes on.

"Another thing," he says. "Our job on the draft board is getting looser and looser the more they need men. At first we had to be halfway strict, I mean the doctors that work with us seeing if the men are fit, as they say. That was in the beginning, but now, about all our doctors got to do is see that these guys are creatures of flesh and blood and not some kind of zombies. The board I'm on sends 'em on to the Army doctors and they do the rejecting, if any. But don't forget, they'll take recommendations from us, the Army doctors will. It's what they call borderline cases, figuring we know these kids all their lives, what they can do and so forth.

"Especially in heart cases," old Masafin says. "If the truth was known, nobody knows about hearts. The docs tell me confidentially they've seen guys got hearts like ninety-eight-cent alarm clocks, fluttering and skipping till hell wouldn't have them. But then again, I got a ninety-eight-cent alarm clock at home, it's the best clock in the house. It keeps going, and that's the way some of the ninety-eight-cent hearts are."

Oh this Mr. Masafin got going all right in his talk with Tim. He finally have another Jameson and he really got warmed up against all this fixing. He almost hollered at Tim, even if Tim had said hardly a word. Old Masafin yelled, "By God, the next guy they try to put the fix in for, we'll see that they take him if he's only a torso! We'll end this trying to fix people out of doing their duty!"

Old Masafin was sore and he exaggerated. But he felt smoother after a while, got everything off his chest with Tim and they had a good talk, all in all, before old Masafin says good night and goes home. He's a fine man and everybody got respect for him for years around this neighborhood.

He left the place, good night, Tim, and good night, sir, and all that, and this night it seems they all seem to come in in a row. First Marty, then Mr. Masafin, and no sooner he left than in come the Man in the Green Overcoat. Listening first to one, then the other, the big idea come to Tim and he went to work on it.

To get it started, Tim began pretty smooth with the Man

in the Green Overcoat. "What would you do in a case like this?" Tim says to him. "A feller that comes in here regular, Marty's his name, maybe you know him? Well, they're going to grab him for the Army, the board'll have him in tomorrow."

"Sure, I know him—Marty Raffernan," says the Man in the Green Overcoat. "They tryin' to grab him, huh?"

"Yes," says Tim. "They are. And the poor guy's feet are none too good and I'm sure he got a bum heart. The Army'll kill him. Do you think you could do anything for him? You're a great man at straightening things out."

"There's lots of cases like that," says the Man in the Green Overcoat, trying to talk like a surrogate or something. "But I'll tell you what I can do. It happens I got a friend on this draft board, known him for years. It's this draft board, is it, the one right here for this districk?"

"Sure," Tim says. "Marty's from right around here, neighborhood kid."

"It's a cinch," Greenie says. "I'll see this friend of mine tonight, I ain't seen him for months, but he'll be tickled to death to see me. Always thought the world of me."

For the time, that was all. Tim said nothing more, just let the matter sink in. Finally, the Man in the Green Overcoat starts out, and when he's going he says, "That Marty won't have to go into the Army any more than Shirley Temple will."

"Fine!" Tim says. He remember later that Shirley's already in, he read where she's an honorary colonel or something.

Inside an hour, the Man in the Green Overcoat is back again. "You come to the right man, Tim," he says. "I got your boy fixed up. My friend—it's old Mr. Masafin if you'll keep it under your hat—he was kind of funny at first. But I talked him into it. He and the board are going to reject this Marty so hard the civilians won't even take him back."

"You're a great man!" says Tim.

"I'm glad to do it for the guy. Glad to do him a favor. Get him all fixed up."

Well, sure enough, late the next afternoon, Marty come bouncing in. He was half-crocked and singing "You Can Win, Winsocki." It's a college song from out West someplace they had on the juke boxes and it was close enough for Marty to a war song. "Bejeezus, they took me! Bejeezus, they took me!" he kept yelling, between "Winsocki" and another jolt of Overholt.

Tim and the Overholt got all the details out of him. Marty says, "I hope the government don't find out before I get in uniform and away to camp, but I think that Mr. Masafin on the draft board is crazy. He kept saying, 'You're going into the Army if I got to stick you together with Spearmint,' and he whizz me up to a hospital for a special examination! The docs up there give me a note to the Army docs about my heart, said it was tricky but it worked."

About a week later, off went Marty to camp. They give him leave to settle up his affairs, that's what they call it. Tim tell me the only affairs is to try and get this girl listen to him a little. Well, she must have listened, because before he went away, Tim and me were going to the newsreels and we bunked into Marty and the girl. They told us they were going to the Music Hall and chop suey afterward. How they made out afterward, who knows about that? God knows I don't and Tim don't.

But out of it all, the Man in the Green Overcoat got the shame of his life. He's not in the saloon for a couple of months, because exactly that time he went up to Rochester to help them make bombsights for big money. But they got wise to him, got sick of him trying to suggest improvements on the bombsights, and back he came. That was two months after he did the fixing.

"How'd your friend Marty make out that time, I could get him a good job in Rochester?" he asked Tim.

"Oh, Marty?" says Tim. "He's in the Army now—was up here on furlough a couple weeks ago, and he looked like a million bucks in the soldier suit."

"The lousy double-crosser!" says the Man in the Green Overcoat. He meant old Mr. Masafin.

A man's going into the Army what can you do about it?

There's quite a lot of finagling along Third Avenue these days because some of the gin mills are trying to steal each other's bartender and at the same time do it in a way that it would not be against being patriotic in wartime. Nobody thought the Army would take bartenders away back when they made that sneak attack at Pearl Harbor, but it stands to reason they'd begin running out of the more athlete type of man sooner or later and they finally did and they finally got around to taking bartenders and now they do, right and left.

That accounts for the bartender famine on Third Avenue. It's not too bad a famine. There's always elderly bartenders but they're usually relatives or else so long in one place they wouldn't move for love or money. Fact is, though, among the bartenders of Third Avenue there's one bartender gone here, another gone there, all off to fight for Uncle Sam no matter how sore feet they got, most of them. Bartenders always have trouble with their feet in the Army or out of it so what's the difference is the way the authorities probably figure it. Might as well have them in, feet and all.

The Army took Paddy Ferrarty practically on its first try at him. His feet weren't too bad. And even if he was swoll up to about a hundred and eighty pounds from drinking now and then over a period of years, it turned out to his surprise he was in pretty good shape.

Before they looked him over, Paddy thought he racked himself for years tending bar always nights, going to bed eight or nine o'clock in the morning and smoking all the time he was awake. But the Army doctors prove to him he had stood up under it all "twenty-twenty" you might say.

Well, Paddy wasn't against going into the Army if they wanted him. He wasn't all hopped up about going, either. Probably that's the way most of them feel about it. Fact is, he edged a little toward the side of wanting to string along with the Army if the Army wanted to string along with him, take him faults and all. He went and had his teeth fixed out of his own pocket after the first examination so he would pass the second, which he did. So that shows he was willing to do his part if they asked him, and they didn't ask him, they told him.

Of course all that's common enough an everyday affair. But it was the way Paddy lit out of this saloon that they'll be talking about around there until God knows when. Those that were there say it was a terrible night in a way and a fine night in another way and those that missed it keep asking the others about it.

It was a Friday night. Being Friday night comes into it because that's when they have the fights in Madison Square Garden and the fights came into this night in the saloon too, the night some of them around here calls now Paddy Ferrarty's Farewell.

When Paddy came in to work that night, the boss was the only one around there knew it was Paddy's last night before he'd go into the Army, report over to Dix in New Jersey, and then on let the Army do the worrying. Paddy had told the boss, but he didn't tell anybody else. He didn't want any stale jokes about it and also he didn't want any la-dee-da shaking hands and good-lucks and all that stuff that's worn out from a couple of wars back.

So Paddy came in and went down to the back of the place the same as any other night. He took off his coat and put on the apron, swung the string around his belly and tied a bow in front the way he had so many years, looking up the bar to see who was in and standing there before he took over. They were about the same bunch as would be there any night at this time.

They got a tradition this part of the city that a night bartender taking over walks the length of the bar making a nod to each one or couple of guys together in front of the bar and saying to them "Good evening gentlemen, good evening gentlemen, good evening gentlemen." It's silly when you look at some of the gentlemen a whole lot less gentlemen than the bartenders that say it, but it's a tradition anyway.

So it might have been an inkling of what he was up to that Paddy went along saying only "Hello, hello, hello" instead of that, and a couple of the customers looked up at the twisted kind of hello Paddy gave them. Then Paddy openly took a slug of Courvoisier, the best brandy there is, now seventy-five cents a slug when it's for sale. Usually when Paddy was whacking at it, he slipped it into a cup of coffee under the bar because it's about nine dollars a bottle and the boss would hit the ceiling if he saw Paddy downing the stuff at that price.

But by that time the boss probably had a hunch there was something in the air, and out he went over to the newsreels. That's the way the boss does when he gets uneasy about anything. He goes hurrying over to the Grand Central newsreel, don't half see whatever is on the screen, just sits in the dark an hour hoping to God whatever is wrong back in the place will straighten itself out by itself while he sits in the dark hell and gone away from it all in the newsreel.

A couple of minutes after the boss went, somebody, a regular at that, rapped a half dollar on the wood of the bar up at the end, hurrying up Paddy. He thought he was hurrying up Paddy. But Paddy walked up to him as slow as a cop walking from doorway to doorway trying store doors at night.

When Paddy got in front of the customer, he stood there, leaned over and put his elbows on the bar, and glared into the man's face. "If there's one thing that's bothered me in twelve years in this joint, it is people rapping a half a buck on the bar," Paddy says. "And you're exactly the kinda guy does it. Rapping money on the bar as if I cared whether I took in your lousy half a buck or you walked out the door and never came in again. Do you think I care about the half a buck from a man that's in such a hurry to swally down another drink? Rap the goddam half-dollar on the bar from now until hell wouldn't have it if you want to, and I'll lean right here and watch you do it! And I hope to God you choke with the half a buck in your mitt!"

The customer was flabbergasted and so was old Rafferty that works for the express company standing next to him. "For God's sake take it easy, Paddy," says Rafferty, meaning no harm.

Then Paddy turns on him, Rafferty that is, and glares him in the eye. "Take it easy, is it?" Paddy says, slow and mean. "And why'n't you take it easy the solid twelve years I been here? Day after day, day after day, giving me a long song and dance about the express company making a monkey out of you, and how you spoke up to the boss there and told him where he got off. The minute you came in that door here every afternoon you got braver and braver about the boss and what you said to him. I can recite it word for word, the stuff you told me about what you said to the boss. 'I told him to his face,' says you to me, one afternoon after the other. 'I told him, look here, you can't make a monkey out of me, I do my share of the work around here and damn if I'll do everybody else's too.' God amighty, am I sick of hearing what you said to the boss. And, truth of the matter, the other guys at the express company told me long ago you haven't opened your mouth there in years. But I had to listen to you twelve years and your barroom bravery about the boss. Take it easy, says you! Well then, will you for God's sake take it easy on those lies to a man has to stand all night behind this stick. Is there no way in God's name you can spare his ears that stuff about you and the boss?"

With that, Paddy wheeled off and bold as you please took another slug of brandy out in the open. He left the two of them flabbergasted, Rafferty and the other guy.

And just then, almost a miracle for the mood Paddy was in, who should come sashaying in but what they call a slumming party in that neighborhood. That's people from Park Avenue and around there, they don't belong in the neighborhood but they're trying to act democratic and having adventures and so on. They're harmless only they're awkward sometimes.

They were hardly up to the bar when Paddy saunters up to them and says, "And what do you quaint people think you'd like to have? Would you care for a quaint punch in the quaint teeth on you? What is this quaint business anyhow I heard you people calling the place a couple of times, and behind my back maybe calling me quaint too?"

The slumming party was looking at each other, and Paddy never blinked an eye, even when he saw the boss come in from the newsreel.

"You're pretty quaint yourself now and then, to my way of thinking," Paddy went on to the slumming party. "Sure the women you have talks worse language than half the men on this avenue and I'm ashamed sometimes overhearing it. And for God's sake do they ever stop smoking cigarettes and littering up the bar with their pocketbooks and stinking the place with their sashay powder or whatever it is. Now, would you like some of that quaint Irish whiskey that I haven't seen an Irishman around here drink in twelve years? Or will you have what one of you people ordered one night, sloe gin and Seven-Up, oh God!"

"Go back and have a bowl of soup, Paddy!" the boss busted in then. He's scared, more or less, of the slumming parties, they're tougher to handle than bums. After all, they're visitors that mean well in their own way and no real harm in them.

It wasn't that Paddy was obedient, but he probably did

feel like some soup that minute, so he walked back. The soup didn't calm him down though. Not that he was riotous mad, though, only having the time of his life getting rid of all the hates he'd been holding in him. It was funny about the boss, the way he took it, only half chastising Paddy, probably because he was helpless anyway. A man's going into the Army what can you do about it?

Ferrarty did the same thing for hours, blasting one after the other of the customers. McLanahan is a man got a small business of his own in the neighborhood and is always having confidential talks with somebody. Paddy turned on McLanahan and told him it was a great pity there was no divorcing among the McLanahans, or Mrs. McLanahan should have got rid of him years ago. "You keep telling me year after year what troubles you have with her and none of them troubles at all," Paddy said to him. "I don't know how they could be because I see her every Christmas Eve you bring her in for a dinner she wouldn't have to cook herself, once a year, Christmas Eve only. And she looks to me like a grand, decent woman, worries herself sick trying to live with an omadhaun like you and not provoke him with some little thing that's no harm at all, like the time she left the step-ladder in the hall fixing the light and you fell over it. To hear you tell that when it happened, the poor woman was plotting to murther you entirely. A woman that'd live with you would have to have the patience of a saint."

And then, by the time the fights came on from the radio, Paddy was well into the Courvoisier. At the beginning the announcer over at the Garden said and you could hear him on the radio, "Ladies and gentlemen, 'The Star-Spangled Banner'!" Paddy stood there with his belly bulging out under the apron you might say and his face got serious and he hollered like a sergeant of the Sixty-ninth.

"Get up out of them booths!" he yelled to the couples sitting at the tables across from the bar. "Get up on your pins, goddam it, there goes 'The Star-Spangled Banner'! Get up or I'll hit you with every bottle on the bar!"

That was the only touch of patriotic that was in Paddy's last night, and by the time he had everyone standing still and "The Star-Spangled Banner" was so long getting finished he felt foolish, you could see. And without another word he had another slug of the brandy and went down behind the partition at the back end of the bar and whipped off his apron. The boss knew it was over, and that he'd have to put on the white coat and go to work himself. So he left off trying to placate the customers' grumbling, and sauntered down to where Paddy was, where hardly anybody could hear them. Paddy was putting on his street coat slow, and his overcoat slow, and fixing his hat on his head at an angle that might show he didn't give a damn even if he was leaving the place for the last time. Well, nobody expected him to do it, the way he'd been acting, but Paddy put out his hand and shook hands with the boss.

"Goodbye, Tim," says Paddy to the boss. "You're not mad at me are you?" "I'm not," says the boss and you could see he almost envied Paddy. "I'm not mad at you at all, though you shouldn't have done it. God bless you, Paddy, and good luck!"

II.

Argument outside a gin mill here

The doll hung above the driver's seat of the truck, which was parked outside a gin mill on Third Avenue— Fifty-first, Fifty-second Street, around there someplace. The rain had soaked the doll, but rain or no rain, it looked gay and lively, a long-legged doll with an orange belly and yellow feet. Hell of a big truck it was too, by the way.

Two guys out of the gin mill were standing there, and one said, "Goddam cute. Looka the doll hangin' up there, will yah?" The other fellow looked but didn't say anything.

The driver's foot was on the step that minute. He was just going to climb up into the seat, but he got down, and in two strides was facing the two men. "Cute, huh?" he said. "Waddayamean cute? Yah mean cute it's all right? Or yah mean cute yah think it's sissy an' yah don't like it? Waddayamean cute?"

The man he spoke to didn't take a backward step. Fairly husky man, who'd go about a hundred and ninety-two pounds, about the same as the truck driver, give or take a couple pounds. "I din say," he answered. He made a face. "Now you ast me, I mean cute yah got about an eight-ton truck there, at lease, and the doll is silly-lookin' on it, now you ast me."

The truck driver's chin came sliding out like the bottom drawer of a bureau. "Silly-lookin', huh?" he said, the words coming slow. "The doll happens to be, if yah wanna know, the doll happens to be my kid's doll. Yah wanna make somepin out of it? Howdya like to get a cute little sock in the jaw for yahself!"

"Aw, whyant you take the truck anna doll an' all an' get the hell up the avenyuh an' be done with it an' nevvamine do I wanna make somepin out of it? I din say your kid's doll look silly on the truck, did I?"

"Chry-sill mighty, yah said somepin about a doll bein' silly-lookin', an' as far as that goes I can take the truck an' the doll an' all up the avenyuh, down the avenyuh, sideways on the avenyuh, an' I can leave it stay where it is, an' wadda you got to do with it? Yah did so say it was silly-lookin'."

"I said a doll was silly-lookin', howmy a know it's yah kid's doll? A kid's doll looks all right an' maybe it's good luck or somepin. It's not the same thing at all as any old doll hangin' on a truck."

The driver considered. He appeared to be deciding not to give up too easily. "I got half a mine," he said, looking at both the men now, "to knock your two cute little heads togedder. You too, yah cluck, yah!"

The last was to the silent guy, who now spoke in a dreamy

way. "I didn't say nothin', nothin' at all, never said a word," he said, in a monotone as level as the top of a pool table. "Holy Jeez, but it's rainin'. The 'L' is soakin' wet. Lookad the 'L,' soakin' wet."

Both the truck driver and the man he had been arguing with stared at the third guy. Then they looked at each other.

"The 'L' is soakin' wet, he says," the truck driver muttered. "Chry-sill mighty, how long this feller been livin' round here worryin' about the poor old 'L' is soakin' wet? The 'L' been there maybe fifty years, been there a hundred years far as I know. An' a dopey bottleneck standin' there inna rain sayin' the 'L' is soakin' wet!"

The big man turned to his chum. "So the 'L' is soakin' wet then. Wad aboud it? The guy onna truck is right! No wunna this country gotta snab oud of it and start getting somewheres. Chowderheads standin' around Third Avenyuh mopin' about the poor old 'L'!" He turned to the truck driver, shrugged his shoulders, and said, "You're right, Mac. Dope is right."

"The 'L' is soakin' wet," the truck driver mumbled, and climbed into the seat and started the truck up the avenue.

Peether is full of blather

On a Sunday afternoon, a hotel room with a dis-attached man in it gets an empty feeling to it, even if it is small and full of things.

By three-thirty, both the *Herald Tribune* and the *Times* crossword puzzles are filled in and lying on the floor. The radio has a symphony that doesn't seem to be the right thing, exactly. It didn't to me, this Sunday afternoon, and I didn't want to telephone anyone, for fear I'd catch them with at least vestigial hangovers and they wouldn't want to talk to anyone, much less have anyone come and see them. I wanted to hear somebody talking, though—and not an announcer, either.

So I went out to get razor blades, which I always arrive at a hotel without, and a shoeshine to fill in the time.

In front of one of the closed stores on Sixth Avenue was a skinny, small man with a pipe, sitting on a pop-bottle box that had a newspaper spread over it. A shoeshine box was in front of him. I stopped there and made a little wordless signal to him that said "Shine?"

He took the pipe out of his mouth, uncrossed his legs and recrossed them, and said, with a bit of hurt pride, "Oh, no, oh, no! I'm not down to shinin' shoes yet!"

The way he said it gave me the idea that for him things were tough enough, but he still had his dignity. He was a lean man with badly worn clothes and sunken-in cheeks, and he seemed to be sitting there as a kind of observer of Sixth Avenue, doing his best to think about something or other but not succeeding very well.

A moment passed and he spoke up again, as if he had not wished to give offense in turning me down in my bid for a shoeshine. "He'll be along in a minyit, the man for the shine," he said. "He'll be along in a minyit. Sit down, if you want."

He shoved over to one edge of the pop-bottle box, leaving some room on it for me, and I sat down without saying anything.

We both watched the people passing by, most of them with an out-of-town look and walking uptown. The skinny man, smoking his pipe, was also watching me, sizing me up, out of the corner of his eye, and I knew he was holding back talk.

"Isn't it awful," he said finally, with his pipe in his hand, "the way they force a man into the saloons even if you don't want to go in there at all?"

He was very sober—I could see that—but he was not a man who had been sober every day of his life. Far from it; the lines and the look on his face told that.

"Well—" I began, not knowing just how to go further.

"Do you mind an hour or two ago?" he said, waving the pipe thoughtfully. "It began spittin' down rain a little. It din't seem it'd last long, but I thought I'd bether go in someplace anyway. I went to the Authomat. Locked! I went over to Bry'nt Park to go into the lavatory. Locked!" He looked straight at me in dismay and went on, "They'd force you into the saloons when it's the last place in the world you'd want to be going! And when I went in there, why, I wouldn't want to be standing there and not buy even a glass of beer, would you?"

"No," I said, trying to appear as thoughtful about the situation as he was.

"Here he is now, the man for the shine," said the skinny man then, pointing with the pipe to an old man coming toward us, a few steps away. The little man stood up and, putting the pipe in his mouth, leaned against the store-front, watching the passersby.

The shoeshine man was well past seventy. He had a bony head, biggish, that seemed too big for the skin that covered it, so the skin seemed too tight for him.

"Hello, Peether," he said to the skinny man, and then sat

down in front of me and slowly got ready for the shine. This small business was most casually run, for the brushes, most of them, were not in the box but on the sidewalk beside it, and the brush with the cleaning fluid on it looked as if it would put more dirt on the shoes than it would take off. When the old man picked up the brush and ineptly began, he looked up at me, and the eyes on him were baby eyes, set in a head older than seventy.

"Well, sir," said the old man to me as he dabbed on the cleaner—mostly on the shoelaces at the knot, and some on the socks, too—"how is the conference making out?"

"The conference?" I was puzzled for a moment; then it came to me what he meant. "Oh, the U.N.?" I said. "I don't know. Most of that is too complicated for me."

The old man dabbed away for a few seconds. "Now, I had the idea," he said, "that a man with a pair of shoes on him like these would know what'd be going on at the conference, if he had a mind to tell anybody."

"No, honest, I just don't know, that's all," I said apologetically, yet giving a proud look at my good shoes.

Peether took his pipe from his mouth and said to me, "Why do all the people want to be going up to Radio City? What do they want to be doing that for? That's where they're all going. Why is that?"

"I imagine they're out-of-town people," I said, feeling

obliged to make some answer. "They read about Radio City and they see it in the movies, and so they want to have a look at it."

"Aw!" Peether said scornfully. "They don't know when to see it at all. It's when them people are all skating around on the ice up there at night and the big lights swashing down on them and some music playing they ought to see it. They don't know when to see it at all. Then it's a beautiful sight, the skating!"

The old man paid no attention as he changed brushes and went on to the polishing phase of the shine. "I'm sure, just the same, a man with these shoes would have a good notion what they're up to at the conference," he said, "and'd know if they're going good at it, or are they all balled up one against the other, or what."

Peether took his pipe out of his mouth again and, speaking past me, addressed the old man. "In India," he said, "they got a pond, or maybe it's a river, that's holy, and they be jumping into it. People that's sick in India jumps into it to get cured." He halted a moment, as if expecting signs of amazement. "And there's dead animals in it!" he went on, almost shouting. "It's full of dead animals, and them jumping into it!"

The old man stopped shining a shoe and looked up slowly at the two of us. "It's the Ganges," he said. "That's what they call it, the Ganges."

"There's dead animals in it, where they jump into it to get cured," said Peether, louder.

"I know, the Ganges," said the old man, and began on the shoe again. Then he said, seeming to address the shoes, "I been all around, a long time ago. I been in Calcutta, I been in South America, I been in Queenstown—they don't call it that any more—and I been someplace else but I forget where it was. The Ganges is what they call it. The Ganges."

Peether rapped his pipe against the side of the pop-bottle box to get the ashes out and took a step or two away.

"Where are you going, Peether?" the old man asked.

"Up to Radio City," said Peether, staring up Sixth Avenue. He looked at the sky. "And if it starts raining again, I'd have to get inside, and I'd have to go into a saloon, whether I want to or not. They force a man into them anyway!" He walked on.

The old man looked up at me as he finished the shine and clumsily shoved the rags back into the box. "Poor Peether is having a terrible time fighting the drink," he said, most kindly. "And when he's trying to fight the drink, poor Peether is full of blather."

"Oh, I see," I said. I gave the old man a quarter, although I hadn't intended to pay so much. He thanked me, and stood up as I began to leave.

"I hope they'll be all right at the conference," he said. "There's bound to be diff'rences here and there."

Atheist hit by truck

This drunk came down the street, walking in the gutter instead of on the sidewalk, and a truck hit him and knocked him down.

It is a busy corner there at Forty-second Street and Second Avenue, in front of the Shanty, and there's a hack line there. Naturally, a little crowd and a cop gathered around the drunk and some hackies were in the crowd.

The cop was fairly young. After he hauled the guy up and sat him down, he saw there wasn't much wrong with him. His pants were torn and maybe his knee was twisted slightly—maybe cut.

The cop got out his notebook and began asking questions and writing the answers down. Between questions he had to prop the man up. Fellow gave his name—Wilson, Martin, some noncommittal name—and his address. Everybody around was interested in these facts.

The blind man in the newspaper hut felt a little put out because nobody was telling him what was going on, and he could hear beguiling fragments of it. "What happen? What happen?" the blind man kept asking, but the event wasn't deemed sensational enough for anybody to run and tell him, at least until afterward.

"What religion are yuh?" the policeman asked the man, who propped himself up this time and blurted out, "Atheist! I'm an atheist!"

For some reason, a lot of people laughed.

"Jeez, he's an atheist!" one of the hackies said. He shouted to a comrade who was still sitting behind the wheel of a parked cab at the corner, "Feller says he's an atheist!"

"Wuddaya laughing at?" the cop asked, addressing himself to the crowd generally. "Says he's an atheist, so he's an atheist. Wuddaya laughing at?" He wrote something in the book.

Another policeman, from over by Whelan's drugstore, where there was a picket line, strolled up. He was an older cop, more lines in his face, bigger belly, less humps around his hips, because the equipment—twisters, mace, and all that stuff—fitted on him better after all these years. "Wuzzamadder with 'im?" he asked his colleague.

"This here truck hit him. He isn't hurt bad. Says he's an atheist."

"I *am* an atheist!" the man yelled.

The crowd laughed again.

"Did you put that down—atheist?" the older cop asked.

"Yuh, I put it in where it says 'religion.' "

"Rubbid out. Rubbid out. Put in Cat'lic. He looks like a

Cat'lic to me. He got an Irish name? Anyway, rubbid out. When he sobers up, he'll be sorry he said that atheist business. Put in Cat'lic. We gotta send him to Bellevue just for safety's sake." The young cop started for the drugstore to put in a call.

"Never mind safety's sake. I'm an atheist, I'm telling you," the drunk said, loud as he could.

"Cuddid out, cuddid out," the older cop said. Then he leaned over like a lecturer or somebody. "An' another thing—if you wouldn't go round sayin' you're an atheist, maybe you wouldn't be gettin' hit by trucks."

The crowd sensed a great moral lesson and didn't laugh.

"Jeez! The guy says he's an atheist," the hackie said again.

A little later the Bellevue ambulance came.

"I yam a natheist," the man kept muttering as they put him into the ambulance.

People don't seem to think things out straight in this gin mill

The way they got things twisted around now, the whiskey firms begrudge you every bottle of whiskey they sell you if you're a saloon. But at the same time they keep giving out advertising and one of the whiskey people gives out a kind of barometer, just a cardboard one, to put behind the bar. This is what started a set-to in this gin mill on Third Avenue the other day. It wound up with a cynic throwing an Old-Fashioned glass into the mirror. An Old-Fashioned glass is one of the worst things you can throw into a mirror, with the heavy bottoms they got. Any bartender will tell you that.

The bartender in this place is named Peter Mugivan and he didn't have much to do this particular time when the barometer argument came up. It was the lull between the noontime hangovers and the late afternoon, when there's the overcured hangovers and the early beginners on the night drinking.

So this quiet time, Peter was standing behind the bar

with nothing much to do and only a couple guys in the place. One was a regular, got a bad temper. They call him Red Barron because he has red hair. He is a cynic, and when he is drunk he don't believe in anything. You can't tell if he believes in anything when he is sober because then he don't say.

Red Barron was standing in front of Peter and this barometer was in back of Peter on the back bar. Red was hung over and he had an Old-Fashioned in front of him all the time.

The barometer is cut out of cardboard like a little house. There's two doors cut out of it and there's a wooden stick on a pivot, so that there's either a woman, cut out of cardboard, can come out one door, or a man, a little tough guy, also cardboard, can come out of the other door. If the woman is out, it means fair weather coming. If the man is out, it means bad weather coming. There must be some kind of chemical worked into it to make it run, but anyway—the woman out, fair; the man out, lousy.

Peter was poking at the barometer and Red was watching him.

"What are you doing?" Red said to him.

"Nothin'," Peter said, but just the same kept on fiddling with the barometer.

"I mean what are you doing to that thing?" Red kept on. He had got out of the hangover enough to want to talk to somebody about something, almost sure to start an argument.

Peter answered him anyway. "I'm shovin' the little guy back in the house," he said. That's what he was doing, and he was kind of picking at the cardboard under the little guy's door with his fingernail.

"Why?" says Red.

"If he comes out it gets lousy outside," says Peter. "Look out the winder, see how nice it is with the woman out the way she was almost three days now. He started to come out about an hour ago. I always keep an eye on the two of them."

"Who started to come out?" Red asked then, because he must have lost track of what they were talking about.

"The little guy here, starts the storms," said Peter.

Red grunted and took another whack at the Old-Fashioned.

Nobody said anything for a couple of minutes. Then Red spoke up again. "Why don't you leave the thing alone? What do you want to mess with the thing for?"

"Oh, I just thought I'd keep him in and let the woman stay out, that's all," said Peter. "Nothin' serious, just fixin' the thing so he can't get out."

Peter was using his fingernail to poke up some of the cardboard so it blocked the man's end of the pivot from getting out the door.

"Well, stop it then, stop it anyway," says Red. "Go on and do something else around here. You're driving me crazy."

"Why should I do somethin' else?" Peter says right back to him. Bartenders get independent now. They know they're hard to get and they talk back more than they used to.

"Aw, for God's sake!" Red mumbled, and he told Peter to make him another Old-Fashioned. Peter did, but he squashed the sugar cube in the bottom of the glass by pounding it, not just pushing down and twisting the muddler on it. He knew pounding it would get Red sore, just like making any small kind of racket would burn him up. Peter must have been a little cross, too, somehow.

"That's enough pounding!" Red barked at him. "Put the whiskey in it and be done with it."

Peter poured in the whiskey and gave the drink to Red, then back he went to poking at the barometer. Red picked the chunk of orange out of the glass and threw it on the floor.

"If I keep the little guy in, it'll stay nice out, like it is now, and I'm off tomorrow," says Peter.

"Listen, you goddam idiot!" Red hollered at him. "That thing, that barometer there, that follows what's going on in the sky, in the air outside, you cluck! That thing *follows* the weather! The sky and the air out there don't follow that thing. It don't get stormy because that piece of cardboard comes out! Do you hear me, you superstitious sonofa-bitch?"

Peter was getting sore too. "What are you hollerin' for?" he said. "I can hear you, and don't call me that. How do I know if you're kiddin'? And I can keep the little guy in if I want to. You don't give a damn is it lousy weather or good weather or what. You don't care about *anything*. I watched you for years."

"Don't tell me what I care about and what I don't care about!" Red yelled. "I do care whether it's good weather or not. But I got some logic, some goddam sense about it. I don't think a bloody piece of cardboard on a stick controls the weather."

"Oh, you know everything, I know that," says Peter, sarcastic, to him. "You know everything, you don't believe in nothin'. I didn't say this little guy controls the weather, exactly—"

Red was getting madder. "He don't control it exactly or not exactly or anyway," he said.

"Hell, I know he don't," Peter growled, "but what the hell harm will it do if I keep him in and leave the woman out like she is when it's good weather? Maybe it'll work, how do you know? Maybe the good weather will keep up."

Red grabbed his drink and gulped it down. "Oh, God!" he howled. "You half believe it! You can't get it out of your head. It's people like you has the whole world screwed up. You can't think, you're bogged down in some kind of Voodoo all your lives, you ignorant—"

Peter flew at him. "Who's ignorant?" he said, real sore, and he grabbed Red by the lapel. "I let you get away with callin' me everything; now I'm ignorant!"

Suddenly Peter let go and his eyes were popping mad. He wheeled around, grabbed the whole barometer, and planked it down on the bar in front of Red. And he pushed the little cardboard guy back in with a twist that bent the pivot so he never would get out again.

"See!" Peter yelled. "He's gonna stay in and the woman out. It's gonna stay good weather and the hell with you and callin' people ignorant."

The Old-Fashioned glass was in Red's hand, and the first thing Peter knew, it whanged past his ear and *bam!* into the mirror. The mirror broke and big cracks ran down into the corners.

Peter rushed around the open end of the bar, at the back. But the cook had heard the racket, ran out from the kitchen, blocked him and held his arms.

Red was staring at the broken mirror. "It's all you can do," he said. "It's all you can do. Kill people as dumb as that. But instead, I busted the mirror . . . Aw, let him go," he yelled at the cook, still holding Peter. "I wouldn't stay in the joint." And he went out quick, through the side door.

The boss didn't come in until an hour afterward. "What happened to the mirror?" was the first words out of his mouth.

Peter only mumbled an answer.

"What?" the boss said.

"Red Barron done it," Peter said. "An Old-Fashioned glass."

"Why? What for?" said the boss. "The last time it cost fifteen bucks. God knows what'll it cost now, the war and all. What happen, Peter, what happen?"

"Argument," Peter said.

Third Avenue medicine

     There's a kind of medicine practiced by old veteran bartenders among old veteran drinkers along Third Avenue, not tourists, and probably the Mayo Brothers out in Rochester have never got wind of it.

Perhaps it isn't exactly medicine, but it's medical observation, anyway, and the main part of it is summed up in two things they say at the proper times. One is "The snake is out." The other, which they say in reverent tones, is "The elevens are up." Neither of these sayings has anything to do with the ordinary, everyday bartender school of medicine, which has to do with overpowering a hangover.

First of all, about the snake. The snake is an ordinary little vein, or maybe it is an artery, that runs along the left temple of a man's head. Most of the time you don't see it, but it's there, and it runs along, a little slantwise, from up around his hair to above the left-hand corner of his eye.

Take a man gets in his late thirties, into his forties, and then, of course, as time goes on, into his fifties, and he still keeps coming into this saloon or that, wherever he always goes, and after a while this vein, the snake, gets to acting up.

One day this man goes on drinking one after the other—nobody is talking about beer but about hard stuff, and especially, out of all, brandy. No use trying to tell him to take it easy; that only gets him sore and he probably says, "Nobody's going to tell me take it easy, I know what I'm doing, I know what I'm doing," and all that kind of guff.

But after a while—and it has to be understood the bartender is his true friend—why, the bartender leans over the bar and takes a good look at him, staring.

"What's the matter with you?" the man probably says. "Have you gone nuts, looking at me like I was some kind of a bug sitting on a leaf? Give me some more of the same. The glass is empty."

"Oh, no, I'm not nuts," the bartender will say, but not for anyone else to hear. "I was just going to tell you the snake is out."

"Oh, oh!" says the man. "The little sonofabitch come out of his hole, did he?"

And he leans over the bar and stares hard into the mirror. Or if he can't see well that far, he's almost sure to go back in the men's room and study his forehead in the mirror. There will be the snake, pulsing and beating away. It must be blood pressure or something.

Time and time again this happens, in a quiet way, and it seldom fails that it halts up the man that's drinking—slows him up, anyway—when no amount of talk or lecturing could do it. Mostly, they come back from the men's room and tell the barkeep they guess they'll take a little walk, and go over to the park and sit for a while, or else they might even go home and lie down. That's what the snake coming out of his hole does, although it's probably nothing serious in the minds of regular doctors.

"The elevens are up" is as serious as anything could be, and there is no joke about it. This is not said to a man to his face at all. It comes about when there's been an old codger around for years and years, long enough to have arguments about is he seventy-one years old or is he up to seventy-eight or even more. Everybody talks of how healthy he is and he can go on for years yet, as the saying has it.

Then one time comes along and he doesn't drop in for a few days or a week. Everyone (except the tourists, of course) asks for him and someone passes word he's under the weather a little. Then he shows up one day, usually when there's only one or two in there. Such a man, in such a fix, hardly ever comes back into the place while the crowd is there. He visits for a few minutes and says he's all right, a little weak, but he'll be all right in a week or so, and then he leaves.

No sooner has he gone than those of his friends who are there—including the bartender, of course—look at each other.

"The elevens are up," says the bartender, quietly and sadly, like a priest or a judge or the like.

"They are, they are!" say the others, and they all nod their heads.

It means that the two cords on the back of the man's neck have begun to stick out, the way they have never stuck out before his illness. The space on each side of each cord has sunk away—wasted, you might say—so the two cords, from his collar to his hair, stick out like two "1"s, making a number "11." That's why they say "The elevens are up" when it happens to an old guy. It means he hasn't a chance and there's not much more time for him. They never let him hear them saying it, but the word passes around, one to another, and for a little while everyone is nicer than usual to the man, until what they're sure will happen does happen.

Hands no good

The big, husky man standing at the bar didn't belong in this saloon any more. There was a time when he might naturally have been there, straggled in like anybody else, but the way this saloon had changed, he didn't fit into it now.

This saloon used to be ordinary enough and on the level. Neighborhood people came in and had their drinks and fights and arguments and talks, and most of them knew one another, and nobody was acting roles like actors. Whatever was wrong with this one or that one, nobody paid any attention to it, because everybody went his own way and was himself, or herself, and let it go at that. Then the place got its name in the paper, and gradually a new kind of people came there—people from fancier neighborhoods and from fancier jobs and business buildings that are full of advertising agencies and the like. The old kind of people felt out of place, and they gradually went somewhere else. The new mob spent more money, and the grogshop got famous. It was always full of people who were trying either to be picturesque themselves or to find other customers who were picturesque, and succeeding in neither. Anyway, few natural people like the people who always used to be in there were ever in there any more.

The big, husky guy might have fitted into the place the way it used to be, but he didn't now. He had broad shoulders on him, made broader by padding. It wasn't a real Billy Taub suit he had on, the kind that Taub makes for leading prizefighters—a "draped" long coat with big shoulders, and flowing pants that taper down to the cuffs—but it was a kind of imitation Taub suit.

The husky ordered a beer, and as luck would have it, there was one old-timer who was standing next to him, an old-timer who had been around a lot and who came in once in a while despite this new mob that was like people wrapped in cellophane.

Even if he was big and battered, the big guy had a sad face on him. His face looked as if it couldn't figure out where the guy would be taking it next.

The old-timer was tight enough to talk to anybody. "You a fighter?" he asked the big man.

"Yeah, a kind of a fighter," the man said. He had a crumbly voice and spoke with queer spaces between the words, as if his throat hurt.

"Was you any good?" the old-timer asked.

The big guy looked down at his hands, folded on the bar in front of the beer glass. He had taken only a little dab of the beer and didn't seem interested in it. He didn't seem interested in anything, only puzzled about everything. "No, I wasn't," he said, crumbly voiced. "I wasn't much good. I was just a fighter. Club fighter, they call them."

"You ain't old," the old-timer said.

"I'm thirty-three—wait a minute—thirty-four now. I near forgot that birthday I had—I didn't get nothing. Nobody gave me anything for my birthday," the big guy said. He picked up the beer but took only a little sip of it, then put it down and folded his hands on the bar again.

"How the hell could you be a fighter? Look at them hands!" the old-timer said. "I never see such little, skinny hands on a grown-up guy."

"What's the matter with them?" the big fellow asked, as if he were trying to be resentful but couldn't. "Never mind," he went on before the old-timer could say anything. "I know what's the matter. They're no good, my hands. I know it. They used to hurt me when I hit anybody."

"Could you hit at all?"

"I could hit pretty good. Only, my hands hurt. Sometimes I pulled back after I got one sock in on a guy. My hands hurt."

"Whyn't the manager do something?" the old-timer asked. "They're little, but maybe he coulda toughen 'em up at that. Soak 'em in salt water, maybe brine 'em tough, somethin' like that."

"I never told him they hurt," the big guy said. "He didn't care a hell of a lot anyway. He just threw me in there with different guys. I think sometimes he thought I was yellow. I don't know, though. I never talked to him about it. I can't fight any more anyway. My cousin says maybe he can get me an ordinary job. I'm living with my mother. She didn't want me to be a fighter."

"Them hands is wrong for a fighter," the old-timer said.

"That's what I say," the big guy said. "But, say, you ought to see my kid brother's hands. Jeez! Big as hams. He can box, too. Maybe he'll be a good one. He's a good kid. I got an idea he'll be a hell of a fighter. You ought to see his hands!"

"Have another beer?" the old-timer asked.

"No, I'm going home," the big guy said. He looked into the mirror as if he couldn't understand his own face, and then he went out.

You can't tell how you'll get clobbered

It was very tiresome on this particular afternoon, because what was the use of watching the ball game on television because no matter what happened that particular day it was going to be the Yankees against the Dodgers in the Series. So most everybody in the bar was merely leaning on the bar and using the drinks in front of them as a flimsy excuse for doing something, if it was only drinking they were doing.

One of the regulars, a former Navy man, had his long blue coat on, because the radio had said that morning it was going to rain and those blue Navy coats shed rain pretty well and he'd been out since hearing the radio. It's a quiet saloon, no chromium or red leather or loud stuff like that, and in the quietness, with no television on, what he said seemed to grab the attention of all of us. He also had been there for several hours and naturally, as a result, was not at a loss for words, as the saying goes. He wasn't talking to anyone, but he was talking to everyone, the way a man sometimes does after a few slugs.

"The sun got tangled up into it, and the jets, and a new

trick kind of paint," he said. "And what happens but a friend of mine gets clobbered. It's like I always said—you can't tell how you'll get clobbered."

The barkeep, not having much to do, had a rye-and-water mixed in front of him and he took a bite of it. Then he asked the former Navy man, "What are you driving at?"

"I'm saying just what I said—that the sun got mixed into it, and how in God's name would you think a pal of yours would get killed roller-skating?"

The barkeep said it still didn't make sense. So the Navy man, with a great show of patience, said, "Let me explain about this, how you can't tell how it'll be when you finally get it. First off, you know they got these jets? Everybody knows that. So the Navy got them, too.

"Getting off the ground, it's a cinch," he went on. "What can you do to the ground? Well, let me explain in case you're not familiar with these here jets. It comes out hotter than blue hell as they take off. So, let me explain, for the Navy they got to take off from a carrier. Right?"

"All that I knew," the barkeep said, with patience equal to that of the Navy man.

"Well, all right," the Navy man said. "They found out if you have just ordinary decks with ordinary paint on them— why, the heat off of these here jets that take off is going to set the goddam ship on fire.

"So that's out. I mean it's out that they could have ordinary decks and ordinary paint on the carriers—see what I mean? So of course the scientists get on the job. So of course they come up with the answer. They come up after a while with a kind of paint or treatment or something that fixes two things.

"Oh, yes, I forgot to tell you, the first notion you'd get, why don't they make a deck out of Monel metal or chromium or something that wouldn't have no paint on it, and how can you set fire to Monel metal any more than you could set fire to a soda fountain that's made out of Monel metal? You couldn't."

He took another slug, and by this time everybody is waiting, without saying anything, to hear what roller-skating has to do with all this song and dance about science and so on.

"So they got to fix at least some of the carriers up for the jets to use them, don't they? Right? So this here carrier my pal is on, why, it's in drydock to get the decks fixed up so the jets wouldn't set the whole ship on fire with that terrible heat they spit out. So what happens? So the kids on the ship find out that this new surface you might say they got on the deck is perfect for roller-skating. How they dope that out, God knows, but kids is kids and they dope out everything, practically.

"Oh, I got ahead of my story. I meant to tell you why couldn't they use Monel metal like in a soda fountain, or perhaps chromium. I'll tell you why. If they did, why, the sun would shine down on this shiny metal and make a reflection in the sky, and if the enemy would see that, it's a dead cinch they'd nail the carrier—you see what I mean? They had to have it like Monel, only not reflect the sun like Monel'd flash it up, that's how the sun got into it. Like I said before, the scientists doped it out, and here was this perfect deck nobody could set fire to, not even a jet, and here was the kids that found out the new science deck was perfect for roller-skating.

"So every day, before they got quite finished fixing up this carrier, why, the kids would roller-skate on it, with skates they got on shore someplace soon as somebody had the bright idea what a good spot it would be for roller-skating.

"Well, to make a long story short, my pal took to roller-skating with the kids, probably to show off he was young as they was. Matter of fact, he was with me when the going was rugged in the Pacific. But what does he do? I'll tell you what he does, he skates right to the end, he tries to make a turn, he can't make it, he goes over, and down ninety-five feet into drydock, and he's killed. It's what I mean—you can't tell how you'll get clobbered."

The television helps, but not very much

When I got into the cab to go down from Seventy-second and Second to Forty-fourth and Fifth, it seemed stuffy, so I gave the handle a twist and let the window down a little.

"That's all right," the driver said. "I'll take and close this here one up, if it's all right with you."

"Oh, sure," I said.

"If they're both open, it makes a draft on the back of my neck," he explained, nicely. "I ought to be home, I got a cold."

"That's about all you can do for these colds," I said.

"Go to bed is the best thing," he said. "Only with me, maybe I'm better off milling around in the hack. Too lonesome home. I lost my wife."

"Oh," I said. "Was it recently it happened? I mean when did she die?"

"Pretty near a year ago at that," he said.

We were moving along Seventy-second, getting near Fifth. Traffic was slow even before we hit Fifth.

Some of them are gabby, the hack drivers. This one

wasn't, even though it turned out we talked all the way. It didn't seem to be gab. It seemed natural talk, almost as if we had known each other a long while.

"I got myself a television," he said. "For company like. The television helps, but not very much, at that."

"No kids or anything?" I asked.

"No, we didn't," he said. "We didn't have any children at all. No in-laws, even. See, we come from another city here. More than twenty years here. We made out all right. It ain't the best job in the world, but we battle along all right together, twenty years. Long time."

"Yes," I said.

"Like I say about the television, I can get interested, all right, like a fight or even sometimes those cowboy movies they put on. Just the same, sooner or later the television got to wind up, don't it? I mean, it comes to the end of whatever the show is or wrassling or whatever it is."

"I know what you mean. The thing goes off," I said.

"Yeah, the thing winds up and there I am again," he said. "I'm alone again and I maybe go to the icebox and get a beer, but it's lonesome. Do you think it wouldn't be so bad if I had kids somewheres? Even if they were grown-up somewheres?"

"I don't know," I said. "I don't have any children."

"They say it's different if you have kids," he said. "Even if you lose your wife. That's what they say."

"Some people say that," I said. "I don't know. Did she die suddenly?"

"She was sick about two weeks, that's all," he said. "But the more I think about it, she must have been sick a long while. The doctor said she must have been. She didn't like to have doctors. Matter of fact, it was me got him finally. And I had to go to him and say to him, look, I said to him, she's going to be sore at you coming in. I said, she's against you before she even lays an eye on you, I says, so please don't mind if she acts sore. Later on, after it's all over, he tells me it was too late, the thing that was the matter with her it was too late to do anything."

"That was tough," I said.

"Thing is I keep worrying," he said. "Was it my fault maybe I wasn't more bossy and make her get a doctor? What do you think? I worry about it all the time. Like that's why I didn't stay home with this damn cold. I'd be around the house thinking maybe we'd be together just the same as always, me coming home and having supper and help with the dishes and we both sit down and have a couple beers, listen to the radio, if I made her get a doctor and never mind how much beefing, squawking she do about it. What do you think?"

"Oh, I don't know," I said. "That's a tough one to answer." It wasn't that I wanted to give the driver a short answer, but there I was, thrown into the middle of a man's life, and I didn't know the man.

"You're telling me it's a tough one!" he said. "Just the same, I got the notion you're kind of sensible, and after all, what harm is there? Like I tell you, I got no in-laws, no kids, I had an idea I'd talk it over with somebody. Them guys around the garage, what the hell, they're dumber than me, even. What do they know? Know what I mean?"

"Yes," I said.

"Like, the truth of the matter, I could get married again right away," he said. "Those guys all said don't be a sucker—don't be a sucker, they said."

"About what?" I asked.

"Well, might as well out with it," he said. "There's this girl I could get married with. Do you think I look forty-eight?"

"I don't know," I said. "I hardly looked at you much. Just got in the cab, hardly looked at anything except that it was a cab."

"I guess I look forty-eight all right," he said. "Well, this girl is thirty-one. She has a little baby. I met her at a guy's house; he had me there eating Christmas. Didn't want me eating in a coffeepot first Christmas I had no wife, he said."

"She divorced or what, the girl with the baby?" I asked.

"No," he said. "Thing is she was a Wac—you know, in the war they had women they called them Wacs. She was in Chicago and she married this fellow, and it's only three months after and he dies on her. So in a little while she had the baby, and that's the way it is. She's a very nice woman, only seventeen years younger. I mean seventeen years younger than me. I told you I'm forty-eight, didn't I? Well, this girl, or maybe I should say woman, she's thirty-one and got the baby and thirty-one from forty-eight, that's seventeen, see what I mean?"

"Yes," I said.

"The guys at the garage say that's too much difference, and with the kid and all," he said. "What they don't understand is I like the kid, see what I mean? I bought the kid a couple toys, and you should see how this girl appreciated it I bought toys for the kid. Don't think for a minute this is any kind of a fly-around dame. She's nice. She lives with her mother now, and she works when she can get work."

"I bet she's all right," I said.

"You can say that again," he said. "Just between ourselves, she proposed to me, you might say. Know what I mean? Honest to God, it ain't this sex stuff, that ain't the main thing at all, no matter what the guys in the garage say; they're always harping about that angle. What I mean is— well, I would like to have her around, kid and all. I like the kid. He ain't very big yet, but he could look at the television, too. Like I say, it helps keep me from getting so goddam lonesome but it don't take care of things altogether, know what I mean? Will you tell me one thing? I mean, I want you give me your opinion—it's pretty near Fortyfourth Street after we get this light."

"O.K., what is it?" I said.

"Never mind the guys in the garage—do you think it'd be all right if we got married? You think it would work out?"

"You're coming at me rather suddenly with this," I said, sparring for time.

"I know," he said. "I don't say I'll do what you tell me, but just the same, you got an idea now how things are, don't you?"

"Well, I think I understand," I said.

"O.K., then, what do you think?"

"All right, you asked me," I said, and drew a deep breath. "I say go ahead and get married. That's what I say, sight unseen."

"Right!" he said, speaking almost loud for the first time in our rolling acquaintance. "That settles it. I guess I only needed somebody, anybody, say go ahead. Like give me a little shove, you might say. I'm going to do it. It's too goddam lonesome. And I like the kid, no fooling. This is Forty-fourth. Do you want this corner or the downtown side?"

"This corner's all right," I said, and got out and hollered back, "Good luck!"

"O.K., doc," he said. He was smiling, and now I guess he'll go ahead and get married. Probably never see him again. I didn't even look at his name beside the picture in the frame, but I hope they make out all right.

This lady was a Bostonian they call them

Little Marty is one of the hackies who play the corner of Forty-second Street and Second near the Shanty there. He has a way of talking that he can pronounce capital letters. If he says a fare was a Society Playboy, why, it sounds as if there was a capital "S" and a capital "P" on the words. One time he was telling about a celebrity that was in his cab and Little Marty said, "They call his folks The Salmon King." You'd know there were capital letters on "The Salmon King."

Another thing. Little Marty has the idea the slightest thing happens to him, it's important. They're not important's a matter of fact, but Marty tells them anyway. Take, for example, here's what he was telling last night having a couple cups coffee in the Shanty, with the cab outside.

"This Lady is twenty-nine years of age—I didn't ask her but she told me her Life History, you might say. She's a Bostonian they call them. She isn't out of in Boston, she lives in a place right outside of Boston, she told me the name, a small place anyway.

"She got clothes looks thicker than the clothes they wear

here. Women, I mean. They cost dough, you could see that. They're tailor-mades—thick, though. More like men's clothes than women's clothes in this city.

"Anyway, no sooner she got in the cab, it's about two o'clock this morning, she Explained the Situation. She don't want to go home, at the same time she don't want to go in and have a drink alone anywhere. That's how it was she put it up to me cold turkey would I go in someplace and have a drink with her, she'd pay for it. I'm not the type guy drinks much anyway, especially whiskey, which you'd have to do, I figure, on a time like this. And another thing, I got no shave and I don't look good—how can I look good wearing the cap? But we're by this time passing a Third Avenyuh place I know one the bartenders and he would know with me there's Nothing Wrong no matter how it looks, so in we go. I know him for years since kids. We went to St. Gabriel's. They tore it down, you know, and put in the tunnel to Queens. St. Gabriel's gone and now they got a tunnel hardly anybody goes through it, they tell me.

"Well, to make a long story short, this is a pretty decent place where we went into, me and the Bostonian. It don't get real Third Avenyuh trade, instead customers comes over from on Park and around there. So when we went in there, the best I could do was braze it out, so first off I excuse myself and slip in the men's room and put water on my hair and plaster it down with my hands before I go back and sit on a stool with this Lady at the bar.

"The bartender was surprise seeing me and a Lady like this popping up but he never blink an eye, too use to see all kinds of things happening all the time.

"Well, the upshot of it was we sat there. The way she told it she came here for the dog show. They had it in the Garden. People come from Boston and Chicago even. It's an International Affair. By the time the dog show's over, there's a week of it, this Lady win a couple prizes. No question about it, she has Dough. An' after a whole week of dog show, why, she stayed here a couple weeks, didn't have to go back to Boston, either her or her husband. The two of them's the kind they don't *have* to go any place, only where they feel like it, they got that kind of dough. I got to say I was surprise she had a husband—somehow I got the idea from the thick clothes she wouldn't have a husband.

"The husband was over in their hotel, a kind of family place off of Fifth, and here it is getting near three o'clock, quarter a three, and the upshot of it was I kept thinking isn't this a hell of a thing now? Nothing wrong, but it was what they call Quite an Adventure for me, even if it got embarrassing.

"In front of the bartender knew me for years, this Lady Bostonian kept saying, 'This is quite a picturesque scene, isn't it? This is quite a picturesque scene.' How could it be a picturesque scene me with no shave, three o'clock in the morning, sitting up at a bar with a Lady I never see before?

"The upshot of it was I maneuver it to get out of there after a while. I made out to do it no hurt feelings all around, but out we got. Then what happens but the Bostonian wants Sen-Sens. I think this Lady got self-conscience-stricken herself at about Forty-ninth Street. She maybe got to thinking about this Husband at the hotel, and so I had to stop the cab and go get Sen-Sens. I don't understand them at all. What's the sense of Sen-Sens and cloves and coffee beans on a wife that's coming in three o'clock in the morning? Anyway, that's all there was to this Bostonian, the end of the matter. At that, she gave me a dollar-ten tip at the hotel, there was only ninety cents on the clock so she gave me the dime and another whole buck. And then with the doorman there listening and all, damn if she didn't say it again, 'It was quite a picturesque evening.' I scrammed out of there."

He should have left him have it anyway

The day hadn't hardly started yet around Second Avenue, so there were only four or five in this coffeepot near Seventy-third Street when I went in to break up an early-morning walk with a cup of coffee and a smoke. Two men from the big beer truck parked outside were having some oatmeal and a couple of eggs. I took a stool near them. They were leaning over the counter with their arms kind of circled around the food and spooning it backward, the oatmeal, into themselves, the way a lot of coffeepot eaters find it comfortable to eat.

The radio was going, not too loud, making a pleasant drone for a pleasant morning. The man on the radio was telling the stories of pieces of music and then playing the pieces. He told about Peer Gynt and played the tune that always used to have bird whistles in it when they played it for tightrope-walking acts in vaudeville, the tune that goes "Deedley dee dum da da deedley doo dum da da deedle dee deedle dee dum."

Not any talking going on, because everybody was busy eating. Then the radio man told the story of William Tell.

He told the first part and then he said, "The Governor then spoke to William Tell and asked, 'But why did you have the second arrow?' And William Tell replied, 'For you sire, in the event that I had killed my son.' "

With that, the beer man on my left spoke up. "He should have left the sonofabitch have it anyway!"

"Huh?" his companion said.

"I say he should have left the sonofabitch have it anyway, making a man do a thing like that, take a chance killing his own son!"

"Who should have left who have it?" the other asked.

"Didn't you hear him?"

"Who? I was eating."

"The announcer on the radio."

"Waddee say?"

"Jeez, you were sitting right there. Just because you're eating's no reason not hear him anyway. He said this king or governor or whatever he was had the whip hand and he made the man take a bow and arrow and shoot an apple off his own son's head. If he ever missed he'd have killed him for sure, how do you like that for a sonofabitch!"

"Oh, I know all about that from way back when I was a kid, I know all about it," the second man said. "What are you yowling about? He hit the apple O.K., never touched the kid, and all's well ends well."

"Maybe *you* heard about it," the first man said, "but I

must have missed it, and I still contend he should have left the old bastard have the second arrow right between the eyes. Don't you think for a minute I wouldn't have given it to him, king or no king!"

"It's only a story, only a story happened a thousand years ago," his friend said. "What are you getting your guts in an uproar for about something happen a thousand years ago?"

"Don't you think I know it's a story?" the first man said. "And I still say hit him with the second arrow and be done with it, there ain't a jury in the world'd convict him. Not a jury in the world! How'd you like to shoot a bow and arrow at an apple on your own son's head? Enough to make anybody nervous and miss the apple, kill your own son stone dead! The dirty sonofabitch, I'm still mad at him."

"Don't get your guts in an uproar, don't get your guts in an uproar," the second man said. He ordered some more coffee for both of them, and then he said, "Tell me this. I been working with you six years, I think it is, maybe seven, something like that. And by Jeez, I never see such a guy for having an opinion about every goddam thing comes up, including bows and arrows now it turns out."

"Are you trying to stick up for a man that would make another man shoot an apple off his own son's head with a bow and arrow, for God's sake?" the first man demanded.

"Naw, naw, naw, naw," the second man said. "I'm only saying something happens a couple thousand years ago, it finely gets around to you on the radio seven o'clock in the morning, and by Jeez, out you come with an opinion on that, too! Somebody ought to leave somebody else have it between the two eyes! And everybody concerned dead as a mackerel!"

"I don't give a goddam how dead they are," the first man said after he gulped the coffee and the two of them started out. "I say and I'll keep saying long as I feel like it, he should have left him have it!"

It's hard to figure how they know

Yanko began first thing by revealing one of the secrets of his trade, which is tending bar in this neighborhood place, where I had dropped into at ten minutes past eight in the morning, right after Yanko opened up, because I was taking a morning walk and wanted to sit down someplace and read the paper before I went back home for breakfast.

He was standing in back of the bar with a woeful look on his face, as if something was bothering him and he hated to start work for the day. He's a large man with a belly, and is ordinarily cheerful enough, but he wasn't looking too cheerful on this particular morning.

I opened up the paper on the bar and it must have been a couple of minutes before he spoke, very weary in his voice. "Do you want to know something?" he asked.

"What?" I said.

"I'll tell you how you can tell any time, any morning, whether I went and got drunk the night before," he said. "It's a secret of the trade, you might say. Look. Lean over. Take a look down at my shoelaces."

I did as I was told, and I saw that Yanko's shoelaces were not tied. In other words, he was shuffling around with the shoes slopping along untied. "They're untied," I said.

"It'll be hours before they get tied," he said. "That's how in the future you can tell any time whether or not I got plastered the night before. Why it is they're untied on those certain mornings is I hate to bend over to tie them. If I bend over to tie them, it feels like the sides of my head's going to pop out on me. So there's how it's a giveaway if the shoelaces are untied, and don't think I'm the only one like that. I know lots of bartenders now and then in the same fix."

To make conversation, more than anything else, and keep him company, so to speak, I only said, "You got a little tipsy, eh?"

"I did," he said, trying to drink a glass of water and only half finishing it. "And on top of that a guy crashes into me with a cab and busts up my fender. Not bad, that's the whole thing. But what gets me is how does my wife know practically everything I do? It's hard to figure how they know, but for once this morning I finely doped it out."

Yanko leaned on the bar and started to explain what he meant. "I'm wearing the windbreaker jacket last night, see," he says. "Well, I got the habit when I'm getting undressed I take all the stuff out of the jacket, all the stuff out of my pants, put it on the kitchen table, where I get undressed when I come in late so I wouldn't wake her up. The idea's I might not be wearing the same thing next day, so I won't forget to put the stuff like change, license, and all that, in whatever it is I'm wearing. I guess everybody does it, anyway I do.

"So all right, I wake up this morning and she's awake already, and first thing, and I'm feeling lousy, but first thing she starts in on me and gives me holy hell for drinking. We get along good all the time, me and the missus, but honest to God I wish she would let me alone for at least an hour in the morning until I pull myself together if I hung one on the night before. She don't. She starts in on me, this and that and this and that and this and that, then out she pops with the remark, 'And you had an accident with the car, too, din't you?'

"How'd she know that is the first question comes into my mind. I ain't awake five minutes, I ain't said a word to her yet, I din't talk to her when I went to bed, I sneaked into bed, and here we are and she's asking me about the accident that happened with the cab and the car. How do you like that for mystery?

"All of a sudden it come to me what might have put her wise. There's a cousin I got lives on a farm in New Jersey, matter of fact he owns this little farm, and time to time he brings in nice fresh eggs, finest eggs you could put in your stomach, right fresh from the farm. He brings them in here to the bar, and I bring them home in the car when I drive home at night. Well, I suddenly remembered I told the missus yesterday morning probably this cousin would come in yesterday and bring in some eggs. That's how I put two and two together in a flash, you might say, trying to quick dope out how she knew about the accident that busted up the fender. What I figured was she was up early and took herself down into the garage where I got the car, only a couple doors from our place, probably looking to see did the cousin bring the eggs and they might be in the car so she could bring them home we'd have them for breakfast. At lease, she could have them, God knows I can't eat yet this morning. Look at the shoelaces! I can't bend down, never mind eat yet for a couple hours."

Yanko stopped for breath, then turned his head and looked vengefully at the rows of whiskey bottles standing in front of the mirror back of the bar.

"Jeez, they must be putting hammers in them bottles, it's all hammering inside my head," he remarked. "Anyway, I managed to pipe up to her and I ask her, 'Were you down in the garage already?' And she snaps back at me what would she be doing down in the garage that hour in the morning. Well, trying to keep peace in the family, I said I thought maybe she was looking for the eggs that to tell the truth I did leave in the back of the car.

"So you see I was wrong when I figured it was eggs and the car and all was how she knew about the accident.

Wrong. So I veered the subject onto some other subject. I asked her would she please lay off me. I asked her as sweet and nice as I could while I was feeling so bad. I asked her please not give me any song and dance so early, before I got a chance to pull myself together and face the music.

"Well, she got busy doing something, and I had another minute to figure out how does she find out about the accident and by that time I was up and getting dressed and naturally I go out in the kitchen and get the stuff, the change and the wallet and everything I left on the table so I could put them in the pants I got on today, not the pants I hung up from yesterday.

"I pick up the stuff and *bingo!* I got it figured out. Because when the accident happen, naturally the hackie that hit me with the cab got out and I got out and we swap licenses, anyway license numbers and all that. And I had it written clown on a piece of cardboard from someplace, 'Sunshine Cab' and a license number, and the guy's name, I forgot what it is, but I have it written down on this piece of cardboard, and there you are! Of course what happen was the missus takes a look at all the stuff on the kitchen table before I was awake, even, and there's this note I took down about Sunshine Cab and license number and all. And I say this for her, she's no dope, she simply put two and two together and she knows I been in an accident.

"I want to tell you it's hard to figure how they know, but

it seems to me there's hardly anything I do, especially that's a little off the beam, that she don't know sooner or later. The only thing I'm kind of glad about is this time, at lease, I finely doped out how she knew about the accident. For once I know, anyway. Most the time I can't figure it at all."

Cluney McFarrar's hardtack

The only trouble with this coffeepot around
168th Street is it's practically one whole war behind the
times. Dozens of guys who go in there off the Fifth Avenue
buses are old Sixty-ninth men and they keep some track of
the war in the *News* every morning. But no sooner do they
talk ten minutes about this war than back they hop into the
other war because it is still more familiar to them. The
result was they got this war into France before it really got
there. They're always talking about Looneyville—that was
a spot in France in the other war—and about LaFurty Mil-
lon they call it—that was also in the other war.

They're bus drivers and conductors on the buses, and
this coffeepot is a hangout for them. Sometimes they get
talking the other war and they get carried away by their
own talk so that once in a while it makes quite a story they
tell, in its own way. The other day it was Cluney McFarrar
talking. He just finished up work on the Burma Road line
they call it, because it's the Number Two that goes through
Harlem.

Cluney McFarrar was a sergeant in the Sixty-ninth and

it is practically a miracle how he weaves around in traffic with that big bus, considering the right arm he got. It was hit by a machine gun in a wheat field and later on he developed a thing in it called osteomyelitis. He knows the medical name for it because he heard the doctors in the hospitals talking about it a million times. But osteomyelitis or no osteomyelitis, he can jockey that bus around O.K., and not only that but with his bum arm he can maneuver the door open and shut in traffic in the twinkle of an eye, so that he can spit tobacco into the street as he goes along. One conductor that works with him says McFarrar is a marvel of timing, opening and shutting the door for this purpose.

This day, a couple days ago, McFarrar finished on the Burma Road, had a slug or two in a place next door to this coffeepot, then came in for coffee and to sit around talking. One thing led to another and McFarrar told about one time in a woods in France—still back a whole war, into 1918.

"There was no more trenches than a rabbit," McFarrar said, "because it was July, around that sometime, and we were chasing them but still plenty of our fellers getting killed. You don't know really what's happening in a war like that until a couple years later when you come home and read in a slow-written book just what the hell was going on that time, like for instance the day I'm talking about.

"We couldn't go up the road, so we were going ahead the best we could through a woods, the woods on both sides the road. They were shelling the road so you couldn't go up it.

"Guys would see Germans here and there ahead of them in the woods, so the way you'd have to do is stand behind a tree and fire a few, then run up and get behind another tree like the goddam Indians they used to have here in this country, except the only Indians most of us knew was those cop-shooters and wild men used to be around the West Side, Tenth Avenyuh and around there.

"That was the best way to do it, behind trees, everybody separated, but it's hell to keep soldiers separated. Or deployed, if you want to call it that. The toughest thing a sergeant has to do is keep the troops spread out, because as soon as there's shooting, they bunch up, usually around the sergeant, which'd make a fine target out of him.

"We kept separated pretty good through that woods, though, going ahead a little at a time. I come across McElroy, from Eighth Avenyuh, behind one tree, smoking his pipe and shooting one shot after the other. He says to me when I bunched behind the same tree, 'Have you got a match, McFarrar? This pipe keeps going out, and I ought to hold up a minute for a smoke anyway. The bolt on this rifle is getting hot, so help me God.'

"All that has no bearing on what I was going to say, I mean about the hardtack. Well, after I left McElroy and ran for another tree ahead a little bit and McElroy found *himself* another tree, I saw something out of the corner of my eye while I was running up to this other tree.

"What I saw was a nice new can of hardtack lying there,

and jeez, was I hungry. I forgot to say the chow wagons didn't get up, and everybody was hungry. And there was this can of hardtack some poor guy dropped. He was dead near it. I had to run past it, but I never saw anything so clear as that hardtack.

"So when I got behind the tree I says to myself, 'I'll come back and get that hardtack if I ever live through this day.' And to make sure where I was, I mean where the hardtack was, I took a good look around. I looked up at how the trees set with regards to the road, and how if a man was walking on the road he could look in and tell this part of the woods exactly. Like distinguishing marks, I mean, that you'd see from the road, how the trees grew and the like of that. 'If it's the last thing I ever do, I'll get that hardtack tonight,' I says to myself.

"Well, the day come to an end, and us maybe two miles ahead of where McElroy and me was behind the tree and the hardtack was."

Then McFarrar said they had a funny thing about that other war, compared to this war they got now. He said in some ways that other war was a union war, like. In some places, anyway, it seemed to have regular hours.

"Near this woods was one of those places where the war kept regular hours," McFarrar went on. "It seemed to stop almost altogether at night, even before night. What you might call twilight, it stopped, only the way I remember it, this twilight come at pretty near ten o'clock. Not dark yet, only getting gray and birds going to bed in the trees.

"The birds were funny. I remember them because when everything come to a halt and I was still alive for the end of that day, I says to myself, 'Now I'll go back and get the hardtack.' And I started all alone back down the road. They wasn't shelling it any more, because whether it seems logical or not, the war come to a stop, I tell you, right about that hour. Not a stop for good I don't mean, but a stop for that day. And I walked back down the road toward the place where the hardtack was. Jeez, I was hungry—no chow wagons yet.

"About the birds. While I was walking back the road, I could hear them loud and busy, getting ready for the night. Banging and shooting sounds all the day, and there were the birds singing or at least talking, at this kind of twilight, as if nothing happened. It seemed funny, and it was that quiet I could hear my feet scrunching the gravel down the road.

"Of course I kept glancing into the woods, so I wouldn't pass where the hardtack was. It got silenter and silenter except for the birds, and gradually they started to shut up and it got a little darker, only not what you'd call dark. For some reason there was nobody on the road but me. The stuff like camions and chow wagons wouldn't come up until real black dark.

"There was beginning to be a little smell from the woods. They were the quietest woods I ever seen then, even though they was certainly noisy all that day we just pulled through.

"I come to the place I marked in my mind's eye, and my stomach give a jump because I knew the hardtack was right in there. Honest to God, I was near starved. I stood a minute in the road and checked up. I wanted to make sure by the shape of the trees I was right and that was the place. And I started to go into the woods after the hardtack.

"Then the silence come over me. Every bird quit all to once. My feet stopped going into the woods. It come over me how in there was all the guys, some of them I knew, would never come out of those woods again. Some of them from New York. Most of them, you might say, because don't forget this was the Sixty-ninth. I thought how they'd never walk around on the New York streets any more, Ninety-sixth or anywhere, and not ever get drunk in New York on Saturday night the way you do. And on top of all that, this silence I got to explain to you but I can't.

"And that was the last step I took toward that hardtack when I thought all that. I turned around and went up the road again.

"I couldn't have gone in those woods if there was Fig Newtons in there."

The fight in the hallway

Leo was sitting at the bar in our neighborhood place with a tall beer in front of him when I went in, eleven o'clock in the morning. First he showed me his left hand, the back of it all swollen, and he asked me to have a drink and I told him too early, and then he announced, in so many words, "I'm waiting for the police to come and get me."

That was a fine thing to run into on such a nice Monday morning—Leo, my friend, sitting there expecting the police. It was a nice morning: sun shining after a night of soft rain, everybody busy around, flowers in front of the flower shop, vegetables, naturally, in front of the vegetable shop, Jimmy, the shoemaker, tapping shoes in the window of his place and spitting nails into one hand like clockwork, with him and the shoe and the hammer all parts of the clock— everything just as it should be, a neighborhood morning in summer near where I live and everything all set for a pleasant day. Well, maybe the niceness of the morning had to be balanced up by somebody being in a jam in the middle of it, as things usually get balanced up like that.

"You bust somebody's jaw?" I asked Leo.

"Big fight in the hallway outside my door," he said. He was twisting and turning his left hand around and looking at it from every angle, as if it was a present somebody gave him and he didn't know whether he wanted it or not.

"I think the guy made a charge," Leo went on. "They tell me somebody said they see him go to the station right after this happen yesterday, and walk in sore. O.K., no use running away. I'm waiting for the police. I'd bust him again. Nobody going to call Joey my 'goddam kid' and tell me keep the carriage the hell out of the hall."

While he was saying this, there were only the three of us in the place, including Yanko, the barkeep, and it was all Greek to me, except that so far I knew there had been a fight in the hall of Leo's tenement. And before I could get it straightened out by listening, Yanko had to go and complicate it by bringing up a fine point of law.

"A cop can give you a ticket for a baby carriage, how do you like that?" Yanko piped up. "What's more, unless I'm mistaken, even a uniform fireman can give you a ticket for a baby carriage, pervided you got the carriage stuck out in the hall, how do you like that? It's a fire law, that's what it is."

Leo got mad for a minute. "This had nothing to do with a fire," he barked out. "Who said anything about a fire? First this guy said something about my 'goddam kid,' that's what he called him, and then started yapping about get the carriage out of the hall. How does fires get into it? Are you nuts, or what?"

"Now, listen, Leo," Yanko said. "You better slow down on that beer, you're getting quarrelsome. That's about eight beers, and it's only five minutes past eleven. I'm not nuts."

"Since when it's your job making remarks how many beers somebody had that comes in and pays for everything they get?" Leo snapped at him.

"Well, all right, Leo," Yanko said. "All right, Leo. All's I said was there's some kind of fire laws that if you leave a baby carriage in the hall, a cop can give you a ticket. I happen to know a friend it happened to personally. He forgot the carriage, left it in the hall, and either a cop or a uniform fireman come prowling along, and he got a ticket. I don't remember exactly, but I think it was a fireman gave him the ticket. That's why I say a fireman can give you a ticket in this case."

I asked them both, Yanko and Leo, would they let the points of law go by a minute or two and clear me up on what happened, what was this fight in the hall. While I was telling them that, in came a woman from the neighborhood with a big basket of what they call damp-dry laundry, and plunked it up on the bar with a big heave. Yanko greeted her by name, and she asked for a beer. Yanko drew her a beer.

"Thank you," the woman said. "We got an icebox full of beer at home but my husband calls it his television beer. If he comes home and gets ready to settle down in front the television, first thing he does is go to the icebox, and if a single can is missing, he hollers bloody murder, like 'Who's been nipping at my television beer? I got that beer for television only.' It's a joke he has, but here I am, lugging laundry and drinking beer in here, with an icebox full at home."

"Was you up at the laundrymat?" Leo asked her.

"Look at the laundry I done," the woman said.

"Was my wife up there? This is Monday. Was she?" Leo asked.

"I was talking to her, Leo," the woman said. "She's up there now. Did you want her?"

"Last thing in the world I want," said Leo, and then turned back to Yanko and me. "Did she give me hell for busting this guy! Ought to be ashamed of myself, she said. But I told her, I asked her was that a nice way to speak about a man's little boy, call him your 'goddam kid,' the way this guy did? She seemed to think that was nothing, nothing at all. Last thing in the world I'm going to do, go chasing up to the laundrymat after her! Anyway, I'm sitting here nice and calm. I'm waiting for the police."

That very instant, Yanko suddenly looks at the door and says, "Oh-oh!" Then he puts his hand up to his mouth and says, a whisper, "Mention the devil!" A cop was coming in.

He was a young cop, a dark-haired man, had a paper in his hand, and he had a friendly walk. He walked in easy, no bullying walk.

"Leo Molik," he said when he came up to the bar. "Anybody here by the name Leo Molik—M-o-l-i-k? Leo Molik?"

Yanko took a swipe at the bar with a rag, never said a word. Naturally, I said nothing. The woman hoisted the laundry off the bar and carried it out, looking back over her shoulder at the cop.

"That's me," said Leo. "I'm Leo Molik." The way he got up off the stool, hitched up his pants, and smiled at the cop, anybody might think he'd been waiting for the cop to come in and give him a season pass for the Giants.

The cop was certainly friendlier than most. He smiled, too. "You don't need to jump up," he said. "Not yet. No hurry. Finish your beer." Leo sat down on the stool again, but nervous. "There's a little something I want to go over with you, Molik," the cop said.

"Yuh?" Leo said.

"Yuh," the cop said. "This man that says you belted him one yesterday has filed a charge against you, claims you socked him on the jaw, no provocation."

"No what?" Leo said, trying to gulp the beer quietly, as if he weren't nervous, which he was indeed.

"No provocation," the cop said. "He claims he didn't do anything to you, and you let him have one on the jaw, that right?"

"He didn't do anything but call my little boy my 'goddam kid' and start shoving the baby carriage down the hall, that's all he did," Leo said. "I ain't going to deny I socked him. I did sock him. Look at my hand, all swoll up."

"I wouldn't brag about it if I was you," the cop said. "Let me see that hand."

Leo held his left hand out, and the cop felt the swollen part and pushed down on it a little. Leo didn't yelp, although it must have hurt. The cop looked at him. "What you ought to do is get some Epsom salts—you can get it at the drugstore—dump a whole box into some real hot water, and soak that hand for a half hour at least," he said.

"That good?" Leo asked.

"Best thing in the world," the cop said. "You don't know how to hit, you realize that? Else your hand wouldn't get all stove up like that."

"It was what he said about my little boy, that foreigner!" Leo said.

"What are you talking about, 'foreigner'?" the cop asked, stern all of a sudden. "Where were you born?"

Leo was all fussed up. "Well," he said, "it's true I was born in the old country, but I'm only a baby when we come here. Look, I been living right here, right in this neighborhood, thirty-four years. The guy in the hall only over here four or five years! He don't even speak English right. Broken English he talks."

"I wouldn't go hollering 'foreigner' about people if I was you," the cop said. "I happen to be a Syrian boy myself."

Leo didn't answer him. He got up off the stool again, hitched up his pants, and said to the policeman, "You got to take me in? All right, then, let's get it over with."

The cop ignored him and looked at Yanko and me. "You know this man?" he asked me.

"Yes, I know him," I said. "He's all right. Leo has a few drinks once in a while, that's all."

"You know him, of course," the cop said to Yanko.

"I tell you, Officer," Yanko said. "Leo got a real good reputation around here, Officer."

Yanko called him Officer twice. Fellows who are not exactly new at explaining things to policemen fall into the habit of calling them Officer every couple of words.

"Thing is, Officer," Yanko said, "Leo here's crazy about that little boy he got. He's what they call an only child. Me, jeez! I got six! Kids ain't any novelty to me, Officer. But Leo here, why he even parades that little Joey in here every couple days, show his new hat, show his new suit or something— Meaning no offense, Leo! Meaning no offense!"

"He seems to go around smacking neighbors in the teeth," the cop said, as if Leo weren't standing right there. "Has he got a chip on his shoulder, or what?"

"No," Yanko said. "It's being nuts about the little boy, Officer, that's the way I'd size it up. I don't know the guy he hit, only of course I seen him around, know him by sight, kind of."

"Look, Molik, I got something to tell you," the cop said, finally. "You realize it's a serious thing have somebody put a charge against you? You could go to jail for a little while, anyway, you realize that?"

"Yes, sir," Leo said. What Yanko had been saying about him seemed to have impressed Leo himself, and he began actually acting like a nicer guy.

"Well, what I got to tell you is this," the cop said. "I have this man outside, the one who made the charge against you. The man you hit. It was him told me I'd probably find you in here."

"He would!" Leo said, surly again.

"Keep your shirt on," the cop said.

"Let the officer talk, Leo," Yanko said.

"I'm not stopping him," Leo said.

"Look, Officer, would you like a beer?" Yanko took a chance and said. "I know you're on duty, but sometimes—"

"No thanks," the cop said. "Molik, you're right, this man outside doesn't talk English too well at all. He can't help that. Barkeep, you know what language that man talks, the one got hit? You claim you know him a little."

"Yuh," Yanko said. "I can talk to him his own language. I got parents the same nationality."

"Well, the thing is this," the cop said. "I figure this a little neighborhood mix-up. I talked to this man, and, best I could figure what he was saying, we can straighten this out. I'm going to bring him in, Molik, and if you get tough, in you go, and I might smack you in the teeth into the bargain. Hear me? Can we sit down someplace?"

"Sure, back in the booths," Yanko said.

The policeman told Leo to wait; then he went outside

and came back in a couple of minutes with the other man. He was a little older than Leo, very nervous, had a look somehow like a professor but husky enough just the same. He was very nervous.

"Come on, Molik," the cop said, and then asked Yanko if there was anybody could tend bar, because he needed Yanko to talk to the man in his own language.

"I get the guy out of the kitchen," Yanko said, and he went back and sent out an old man who helps out in the kitchen. The old man could fill in for a few minutes, anyway, behind the bar. The cop said I might as well sit with them if I wanted to, and so I did, all of us in the booth.

The man that got hit had only a small swelling on his jaw. Leo's hand was hurt worse than the man's jaw was. The man got more and more nervous every minute. All of a sudden, he pawed at all his pockets, and finally found a handkerchief and pulled it out, because he was crying. Big tears.

"What's the matter with him?" Leo piped up. "What's the matter with him? It's me that's in trouble for hitting him. What's he crying for? He's in the clear."

"Take it easy, Molik," the cop said. "*You* ask him what's wrong, what's he crying for, Barkeep."

Yanko spoke to the man in whatever language it was. He seemed to be asking him a long question, a lot of words. The man aimed all his answers at Yanko, and he didn't stop crying but he talked and talked and talked, none of us except Yanko knowing what it was all about. Then, little by little, Yanko would hold his hand up and stop him and tell the cop and Leo and me what he said.

"He says he was sorry all night and couldn't sleep," Yanko said. "He says he cried at night, too, on account what happened. He says he don't want no harm to come to anybody, and where he got hit don't hurt any more."

The man talked some more and more and more, and every once in a while Yanko had to stop him and explain.

"He says he forgot himself altogether, that's how it happened he said bad words, that's what he said, bad words, about Leo's little boy," Yanko explained. "Here's what he says. He has a wife and a little boy in the old country and he come over to this country try to make enough money bring them over here to be with him. But he says he can't make the grade. I mean that is what it amounts to in English, he can't make the grade."

The man talked some more, very intently, to Yanko, as if the rest of us weren't there.

"He says it's true he had a few drinks himself before the fight they had in the hallway," Yanko said. "He says it's true he did. He says when he drinks, all he thinks about is how too bad it is he don't have his wife and baby here like everybody else has their wife and baby. He says he don't know why he got mad and called him 'goddam kid,' he says, except he says everybody got a wife and little boy except him. He's very sorry all night last night and can't sleep because the fight happened."

The man broke in on Yanko. Putting his handkerchief away, the man said to the cop, in English not too bad at all, "I don't want anything should happen with the police to Mr. Molik. I am sorry I go to the police station. I forgot myself altogether, and I tell Mr. Molik before you this little boy is a good boy. He is not goddam kid, like I said when I forgot myself. He is a good, nice little boy, like my little boy used to be. I do not want anything should happen to Mr. Molik with the police. Is all right, sir?"

"Everything's O.K.," the cop said.

He asked Leo and the man if they would shake hands. Leo didn't say a word. They shook hands, and the cop got to his feet. He and Yanko and I went back to the bar.

The cop stood there a minute. "Hard luck, the man having his family stuck on the other side," he said to Yanko.

"Yuh," Yanko said. "You still don't want a beer?"

The cop said no and started out.

"Before you go, Officer," Yanko said. "A cop can give a ticket for a baby carriage in the hall, can't he? It happen to a friend of mine."

"Yes. It's a fire-law violation," the cop said.

"How about a uniform fireman, he can give a ticket, too, for that?" Yanko asked.

"The inspectors usually report it and something's done," the cop said. "Well, I got to get going. So long!"

An old college chum

The cab I took at Seventy-second and Second was driven by a lean, easy-smiling man of about my own age, which is getting along up there. Although he was not forcibly gabby, as so many hackies and quite a few passengers are, we did start talking. Perhaps I started the talk, making some remark about the Giants, because I'd been watching them on television alone in the house a few minutes before. I'd had nobody to make remarks to about some of the more startling plays, and it is almost impossible for me to watch a ball game, on television or in real life, without making remarks to somebody. There's no "perhaps" about it, I did start the talking, going over west on Seventy-second.

When we got down to Park and Fifty-fourth or Fifty-fifth, somewhere in there, a red light pulled us up, over near the island that's in the middle of Park, and there was a traffic policeman on duty there. It was drizzling some, and he had on his heavy black raincoat and his black rain hat. We were the front car in the stopped line of traffic, and so not far from the cop.

He was a fairly grim-faced cop, but when he glanced over and saw the man driving my cab he gave a big grin. "Hi!" he hollered to my cabby, as the crosstown traffic drifted by easy for a moment.

"Hi!" the hackie answered, leaning relaxed out the left-hand window. "How you doing?"

"O.K.," the cop answered. "How you making out these days?"

"Not too bad, not too bad," the cabby answered, and then the light went green, the cop waved us all on, and we started down Park again. I could see the hackie looking at my reflection in the rear-vision mirror. I got the idea he was expecting me to say something.

"Friendly kind of cop," I said.

The driver laughed. He had an unobtrusive, easy laugh. "He's an old college chum of mine," he said.

I hadn't heard the expression "an old college chum" for years and years. It's an old-timey expression, but then, as I said, the driver and I seemed to be about the same age, neither one of us a kid.

"College?" I said.

"Well, that's a kind of a gag," the driver said. "I mean we graduated from the Police Academy together. Way back in 1923. Never forgot each other."

That stopped me for a few seconds, not wanting to be nosy. But I could see the hackie was still watching me in the rear-vision mirror, so I asked him how come he wasn't on the cops, too, or did he go on and retire or what?

"No," he said. "I almost got on the cops but I didn't." He quit smiling and laughing. He seemed to be figuring whether to go on or not, far as I could tell in the mirror, and then he half turned around as we stopped at another red light.

"You went into something else, huh?" I asked.

"I had to go into something else," he said. "But I wanted to go on the cops, like him. I lost out on going on the cops. It's a funny thing, what happened. I think of it every time I see him, and I guess he thinks about it, too. One day we talked about it, Labor Day I guess it was, hardly any traffic and I was riding empty. No use making any bones about it, it doesn't make any difference any more anyway. What happened was they found out I had a petty-larceny rap. A black mark on me. That ended me with them."

The way he talked, the hackie seemed neither resentful nor regretful either, merely thinking about it, brought to mind by the cop hollering "Hi!" The light changed, and we went on.

"I was only a kid and I was delivering groceries," the hackie said. "I went in a house with groceries, and there was nobody in the kitchen and I saw a watch on a table and I took it. Might as well say the truth, I stole it. It doesn't make any difference any more.

"I don't understand what small things a guy remembers

when he gets to be our age," the driver said. "I remember it was what they call a 'gold-filled watch.' Course, I know that means the case was gold-filled, what I mean, only part gold. Why I remember is after they caught me and the time came they read out the charge on petty larceny, the guy read out 'gold-filled watch' and I remember thinking then, kind of daffy, about a watch filled inside with gold instead of works.

"Well, that had nothing to do with it, it's only that I never forget about the gold-filled part. What the hell, I was only a kid when I did it.

"Thing was, when I took the examinations for the cops, I didn't put it down about the petty-larceny rap. I was a man then, and honest to God I forgot all about the watch thing that happened when I was only a kid.

"That was it. Maybe if I had put it down, they would have overlooked the whole thing. But they found out on their own hook, they look you up matter of routine, and they found out about the watch. From then on, it was no go with me. I made a good mark, too. I got an eighty-eight and two-tenths, it was. That cop you saw on Park, he got the highest in the class, or pretty near it, he got a ninety-two and something."

It seemed to be my turn to speak, so I said, "And he's still on traffic, with a ninety-two and on the cops all this time since 1923?"

"That's the way it works out," the driver said. "Still on

traffic, him, and still pushing a hack, me. That's what we were talking about that Labor Day or whenever it was we talked.

"Still and all, we aren't so bad off, either one of us, that's what we said that Labor Day or whenever it was. Funny thing, after all these years he seemed more sorer than I was after all these years about them holding that watch against me and not letting me get on the cops the way I wanted to get on. He said a couple of times it could have happened to any kid. Kids don't have to be bad to do a thing like that all of a sudden, take a watch from a kitchen table delivering groceries.

"You don't have to believe me. It doesn't make any difference whether you do or not. But honest to God, that watch was the only thing wrong I ever did in my whole life. No, I don't mean that, I did plenty things wrong, I mean that was the only thing illegal, stealing, I ever did in my whole life before the watch or since the watch. That cop up there'd tell you the same thing, never was in a jam, I mean a criminal jam you might say."

We were getting near where we were going in the cab, and the hackie stopped talking for a minute or so. I could see him grinning again in the rear-vision mirror.

"Oh, what the hell, it work out all right after all," he said, before we stopped at the curb, on West Forty-first. "That's what we said that Labor Day or whenever it was. He asked me did I still wished I had got on the cops and I told him sometimes I did, and what does he say but he sometimes see me go by and wished he was a hackie. Turns out I got a wife and family, two good kids, both boys growing up and I make out all right, and he got a wife and family, he got two girls and one boy and he says he's doing O.K. It work out all right when all is said and done."

Tell him what happen, Joe, see will he believe you

Three Italian boys were standing together down at the far end of the bar this sunny noontime when I went in our best neighborhood gin mill for a beer. It was very hot.

I knew two of the boys—neighborhood guys, they were—and the third one, slim, and in his twenties, I didn't know. He was a stranger, but he had something of the same look of the two fellows I did know. I couldn't quite make out what they were doing while I stood nearby and had my beer. There were three of them, as I said, but they had four glasses in front of them, all beers. One of the boys would take the fourth glass and from it he would pour a little sip of beer into each of the three other glasses, and then the three of them would lift up their glasses and drink a tiny bit of beer like a toast. I couldn't figure it out, especially because it didn't seem like some kind of gag; all three of them were sad-looking to a certain extent.

Usually, if I happened to bump into those two of the three that I knew in there in the saloon, why, we'd right away begin gabbing about the Giants, or the Yankees, or the horses, or something like that. But while this pouring beer little by little out of nobody's glass, as you might call the fourth glass, went on, there wasn't any gab at all, outside of my two friends nodding hello. Eventually, though, they finished the beer, fourth glass and all. The one they call Vinny, his name is Vincenzo, beckoned me to move over and join them, and he must have noticed me looking at the fourth empty glass as if I was wondering what the hell was going on, which I was.

"We're drinking the old man's beer," Vinny said. "You was away from the neighborhood a couple days, wasn't you? I guess you didn't hear we had our old man die on us?"

"No, I didn't hear that," I said. "I'm sorry."

"We just come from the funeral," Vinny said. "This here is Al, my other brother, you never met him."

Al was the third man, the one I didn't know, of course. We shook hands and I said something again about being sorry for his father dying. He said "Thank you," and asked me if I would have a beer, as they were signaling Johnny, the bartender, for another round, no extra glass this time.

"We were making out the old man was here with us," Vinny said. "So we had Johnny pour an extra glass of beer and we all drank some of it, you seen us. I figured you were wondering what was it all about. It was like having him here with us. He liked a glass of beer, the old man did."

We all took a little swig of the fresh glasses of beer

Johnny poured out, and Vinny said, to me as well as to his two brothers (the third one's name is Joe), "He sure was here with us all right, wasn't he, Joe?"

"I can't help thinking he was," Joe said. "Especially after you think what happen, he sure was. Don't you think so, Al?"

"I know he was," Al said.

"Al comes from Haverhill, up in Massachusetts," Vinny said to me. "He come down for the funeral. We just come from the funeral, it's all over. Al got to go back to Haverhill. That's where he lives, Haverhill."

There was something else in the air. I didn't know what it was, the next minute or two, because nobody was saying anything.

"Tell him what happen, Joe, see will he believe you," Vinny said suddenly. We waited for Joe.

"The old man was a shoemaker," Joe said. "Well, we're driving to the church in my car, this is only a couple hours ago. So when I'm going fast, like on Second Avenue, I keep hearing something go tap, tap, tap on a wheel somewheres. I don't say anything, because I think I'm going nuts maybe. Tap, tap, tap on the automobile wheel, and it's like when I'm a kid listening to the old man going tap, tap, tap on a shoe when he's working. The old man was a shoemaker, like I told you.

"Anyway, I get to the church, I mean we all get to the

church, all in my car, Vinny and Al and me, and we have the old man's funeral. So after a while it's over and you won't believe what happen. What happen is after it's over and I go look at the tires and the wheels, and Vinny I think it was, maybe it was Al, ask me what's the matter. I told them I thought I heard some kind of a noise like a tap, tap, tap, like, on our way to the church with the old man like him tapping shoes. Al or maybe it was Vinny says by Jeez he heard it, too, on the way to the church. So I was relieved when I heard them say that, because I wasn't too sure did I really hear that noise or was I going crazy.

"Well, I got around to look at the far-off wheel on the back, the last wheel I looked at, and what do you think was stuck into the tire? It was a tap, I mean like the bottom lift off of the heel of a shoe. It was stuck in the tire. The old man was a shoemaker, and here it was, a bottom lift off of the heel of a shoe, like God knows how many thousands of things like that the old man in his life tapped onto shoes. That's what was stuck into the tire and it should have punctured the tire and it never did."

"The old man sure was with us all right," Vinny said when Joe had finished. "No kidding about that, the shoe-maker piece of leather stuck in the tire and all!"

Then he turned to me and asked, "Do you believe it, what happened?"

I said of course I did.

"Well, Al got to get back to Haverhill—eh, Al?" Joe said.

"Yes, I got to get going," Al said. "I bet they won't believe me in Haverhill when I tell them what happen. The old man being right with us, I mean, tap, tap, tap all the way to the church."

NOTE

"This Place on Third Avenue" and "They Don't Seem to Be Talking to Grogan" are published here for the first time. The other twenty-six stories first appeared in *The New Yorker.*

Sixteen of these stories were collected by the author in his book *Third Avenue, New York* (1946). Two more, "Third Avenue Medicine" and "The Television Helps, But Not Very Much," were collected in *A Man Gets Around* (1951). After the author's death, most of these stories, plus "Peether Is Full of Blather," "Hands No Good," "It's Hard to Figure How They Know," "The Fight in the Hallway," "An Old College Chum," and "Tell Him What Happen, Joe, See Will He Believe You," were reprinted in *The World of John McNulty* (1957), an omnibus edited by Faith McNulty. "You Can't Tell How You'll Get Clobbered" and "He Should Have Left Him Have It Anyway" are collected here for the first time.

"This Place on Third Avenue" is adapted from the "Description of the Set" that prefaces *What Goes On Here,* a play based on the Third Avenue stories written by McNulty and Philip Dunning in 1942–43. The play was never published and never produced.

"They Don't Seem to Be Talking to Grogan," like *What Goes On Here,* was found among the author's personal papers, now in the possession of Faith McNulty. The typescript is undated, but the story was written before the summer of 1942, when "Man Here Keeps Getting Arrested All the Time," the first of the published Grogan stories, appeared in *The New Yorker.*

FAITH MCNULTY

Faith McNulty was born in New York City in 1918, the daughter of Judge Joseph E. Corrigan and Faith Robinson Corrigan. After two years at Barnard College she went to work in journalism, first at the New York *Daily News* and later at *Life* and *Collier's*. In 1944–45, she served as a writer in the Office of War Information in London. Upon her return to America, she married John McNulty and began to contribute to *The New Yorker*, eventually joining the staff in 1953. For *The New Yorker* she has written short fiction, The Talk of the Town, Notes and Comment, and an annual children's-book column, but she is best known for her remarkable reports on animals, especially endangered species. Among her books are *The Whooping Crane* (1966), *Must They Die? The Strange Case of the Prairie Dog and the Black-Footed Ferret* (1971), *The Great Whales* (1974), and *The Wildlife Stories of Faith McNulty* (1980). She is also the author of *The Burning Bed* (1980), an account of the case of Francine Hughes, a battered wife who murdered her ex-husband. In recent years she has devoted most of her writing to natural-history stories for young readers. She lives on a farm in Wakefield, Rhode Island.

MORRIS ENGEL

Morris Engel, a lifelong New Yorker, was born in Brooklyn in 1918. In 1935 he joined the Photo League, where he studied both film and still photography with his mentor Paul Strand. In 1940 he was briefly on the staff of the newspaper *PM* before joining the U.S. Navy's Combat Photo Unit No. 8. Capt. Edward Steichen, in a Navy Citation for Exceptionally Meritorious Photography presented to Engel in 1945, said "his photograph showing enemy dead on the Normandy Beach, taken on D-Day and in the face of grave danger, is one of the great pictures of the war." After the war Engel returned to *PM*, for which, in 1947, he took the pictures of John McNulty that are reproduced in this book. In 1952–53 he made, with his wife, the photographer Ruth Orkin, his first feature film, *Little Fugitive,* which François Truffaut credited with revealing to him the possibilities of the independent cinema. Since then his work has been a fluid journey between his three chosen media—photography, film, and, in recent years, hand-held video.